Societal Suicide

Julián Segura Camacho

Hamilton Books
A member of
The Rowman & Littlefield Publishing Group
Lanham • Boulder • New York • Toronto • Oxford

Copyright © 2006 by
Hamilton Books
4501 Forbes Boulevard
Suite 200
Lanham, Maryland 20706
Hamilton Books Acquisitions Department (301) 459-3366

PO Box 317
Oxford
OX2 9RU, UK

British Library Cataloging in Publication Information Available

Library of Congress Control Number: 2006925773
ISBN-13: 978-0-7618-3514-1 (paperback)
ISBN-10: 0-7618-3514-8 (paperback)

∞™

Dedicated to

Geronimo

A person rarely recognized as a Mexican who fought for his home
and his identity, actions which protect us from this societal suicide society.

And to
Apacheria,
The Apachis' Homeland—
a land severed in Two

Mire ayjado, yo entiendo que este es su país, pero el Americano es maldito.
No hay que hacerse como ellos pero hay que saber sobrevivir.
Aqui estamos, que vamos hacer?

Son, I understand this is your country, but Americans are evil.
One must not become like them but you must know how to live among them.
After all, we do live here; what are we to do otherwise?

—Gustavo Magaña, My Paternal Abuelo (1922–2005)

The farther my people keep away from the Whites,
the better I shall be satisfied.
The White people are wicked.
I want you to teach my people to read and write, but they must not become
White people in their ways.
It is too bad a life, I can not let them do it.

I would rather die an Indian than live a White man!

—Sitting Bull

Contents

Contents

Acknowledgments

I want to thank those who read individual chapters as I emailed them for opinions and others who helped in other ways: Angel Medina, Cuco Aguilera, Roberto Negrete, Reuben Lopez, Marcos A. Ramos, Maricelia Carmona, Oscar Barajas, Jose Mungaray and Ruben Puente. A special thank you to Socorro Natividad.

Most importantly, I want to say mil gracias to my editor Joanna Camacho for aguantando my demands. You have made these words walk and talk like a dream revealing itself.

Introduction

Societal Suicide is a compilation of factors, experiences, realities and contradictions of life in California, specifically in Los Angeles. The stories are not about a simplistic life but about the issues that make one suicidal both from a societal and a familial perspective — both of which are interlinked.

My writings are always Mexican based — that is Mexican but not defined by Mexican Nationalism or a south of the border view of the world. This body of work can only exist in an American construct, a construct resulting from American power and fortification of a border. In *White By Law: The Legal Construction of Race*, Ian F. Hanley Lopez validates the stories I write about this suicidal society: "In the prerequisite cases, we may assume violence, probably literally in the corporeal forms of immigration officers and border guards, certainly figuratively in the form of constrained lives and truncated hopes, and occasionally obviously in the form of suicide" (page 121).

Mexicans in the United States, irregardless of birth place, are forced to live suicidal tendencies. After all, we are socialized and educated on this side of the border. The American caste structure imposed on me and other Mexicans triggers these feelings of suicide

Simultaneously, I do not profess to write about all Mexicans in the United States, especially those Mexicans who believe that they have benefited by being in the US or those who have a positive view of the US based on employment and weekly carne asadas.

I know no other life than that of having been born in California and raised in Los Angeles County. I only know a Mexican life in Los Angeles. And, after thirty six years of existence, I know what aspects of American life drive me to be suicidal. Merely thinking about American society: exclusion from a good quality neighborhood; inequitable education; unfair advantages given to Whites, White females, White Blacks, and now White Asians; and the hypocrisy of American success make many of us suicidal. How many of us subsist is a testament to the will to survive, especially in a cultural space that never intended to include me and many other Mexican Apachis.

At times I think suicidal, but my inner voice, Ehecatl Miquiztli (The wind of death), tells me inside that that would mean that America won, and I cannot allow them to determine when I leave. This also means that just as I am suicidal, this society drives itself to think suicidally because it fuels a negative backlash toward Mexicans, not a violent backlash but a spiritual death where it will find itself not able to escape the grasp of its own evil deeds. These stories are about unhappiness in the land where I belong but am not accepted nor see hope.

Some might dismiss these words because of the negative connotation, but these stories contain a mere revelation of the truth. These stories reveal the way America resides in truthfulness, not the way America pretends to be.

This is la chingada society, a social order that attempts to abolish the Mexican to save itself. La chingada society is America at its best in my opinion. Why can't the truth be read and spoken even if it ruffles the feathers? Do we not all have a stake in the advancement of this hellhole?

Not committing suicide originates from these words, these words release such repression.

Chapter One

Adobe

El Rancho Roa, Mexicali, Baja California, 1973–1974

My apa, Matias, always respected the sun by wearing sombreros. He wore sombreros all his life, from Pachuco L.A. style with short felt rims to straw hats with tourist circus sombreros, which had "Mexico" sewed on, as if he forgot that he lived in Mexico. The Sonoran desert sun never let him forget he was in Mexico though; his Mexico was California. Looking north from his sombrero, he could see the Sierra Juarez become the Cleveland National forest or the Tecate Divide on Highway 8. All of it was Mexico. It was one long spinal cord for the body of California; the sun equally burnt both sides.

Still, my apa knew he was in Mexico because in Mexico you could build your own house not with wood or brick but with adobe. Adobe was the material my grandparents' house was made of. Adobe was clay, soil, and mud—earth—transformed into blocks and placed vertically upward towards the sun. The adobe made the earth seem upside down. Generally, a person walks on the earth; here though, the tierra was perpendicular to the tierra. The tierra extended upward as one continuous body of clay and was separated by the wood frame of the block and the hay mixed into the adobe.

I remember my apa behind the alamo tree, shade from the powerful sun mixing clay and straw in a bucket. I squatted next to him, four years old as if to know what he was doing, really just being metiche. He was on his knees mixing the watery soil with the yellow straw creating the dark chocolate brick. He mixed with his hands and forearm: back and forth, back and forth in circular motion. I could see the clay line in the middle of his arm as if the adobe was dressing him. He hustled to make enough blocks; he only had two rows of adobe blocks drying and sweating from the heat of the sun. He wore a short sleeve cotton plaid shirt that was buttoned only at the middle

1

Figure 1.1.   "Adobe"

of his stomach line, covering the side to side scar he had from gall stone surgery ten years prior.

Once the mixture was ready, he poured the adobe into a wood molding on the ground with the force of his body, all the while perspiration dripped into the bucket as if to anoint the house. The wood molding was an 8 by 10 inch block frame, two inches thick. Slowly and patiently, he would dispense the mixture into the molding with the ground being the backdrop. He would fill it carefully not to overflow and then spread out the adobe evenly.

I watched and admired him build his home in my innocence. His work seemed endless and tiresome since the sun pierced boldly without pause. Hour after hour, more adobe blocks were laid out to dry. The sun was his friend, for the sun would dry his wet adobe.

I always considered myself lucky because I saw my apa build his home. In Inglewood, we did not live in an adobe home, but somehow the adobe home that my grandfather had constructed through the 1950s, 1960s into the 1970s seemed like my real home. I remember him taking the dry adobe blocks and stacking them from the ground up with his sombrero on and the sweat dripping down his face. By the time the add-ons were complete, the old adobe bedroom was solely a storage room.

Yet, that mere storage room told a story of the past, for anyone could see the oldness in the decaying and colorless clay. The room was large enough to fit two full-size beds, a foot-peddle Sears sewing machine, and a hanging crib with an entry point to a second albeit smaller bedroom. My apa built his home, a home that some might define as a poor man's house because it had a dirt floor and no electricity; however, this house was his labor, his love, his expansion for the grandchildren who would visit him or his renovation, a fixing up of worn out parts that were ready to return to their origins.

Somehow that adobe house seemed more like my home, more than the Inglewood house, which we knew belonged to somebody else because he showed up every month. I never saw my father built the one bedroom unit in Inglewood. I knew that was not our place.

The adobe home could be built from the ground up by my abuelo; it was a place for living, eating, breathing, and playing with no one telling us we were making too much noise.

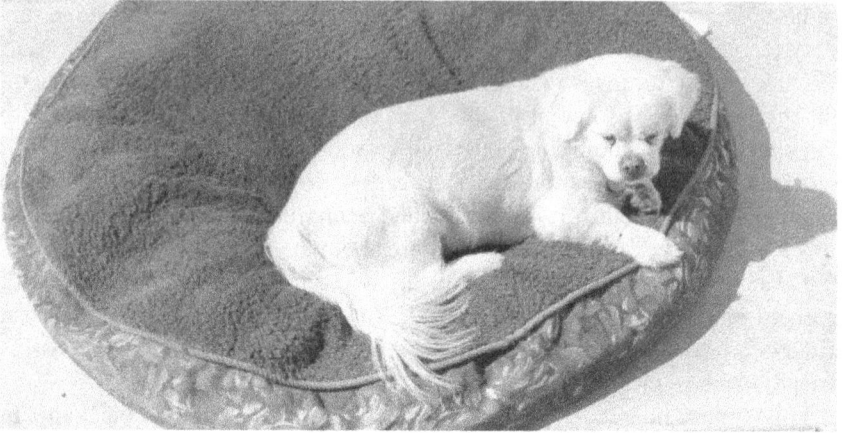

Figure 2.1. "The Pekinese Napping"

Chapter Two

La Siesta

Before the United States invaded northern Mexico, Mexicans of California engaged in an important ritual after a long day of work which began early in the morning before the sun turned hot: La siesta.

In rancho days, whether milking cows, tending to the pigs and chickens or picking cotton (as I once did as a teenager in Mexicali), people saw that after a long morning of work, a break was needed. That break was a return to their home or if not, a long nap on top of a cobija most carried, under an alamo shade.

The nap was brought on by a meal of chorizo tacos con frijoles and cold water. It was relief from the pinche sun. The break was needed after almost six hours of straight work. Sweat would dry on your skin and off to the roncos you went.

I remember my grandfather would sleep on top of a costal, potato sack or a cardboard box in front of his adobe home; he'd take his shoes off, place his sweaty sombrero to one side and curl up right next to his perspiration. I always thought it was strange, but this viejito returned to his fetal position and did not care about life or intruders during his siesta. Poor he was not, he had his bed in his adobe home, but the shade from the willow tree and the adobe house seemed to be cooler.

Pobre no era, he was taking his siesta. How could he be poor? The man slept after his honorable five hours of hand milking cows. After two hours of rest, he was up and ready to return to the evening shift—refreshed and protected from the intensity of the heat. And off he dragged his feet back to work.

Siestas were great relaxers, energizers, replenishers of life. A person seemed to die in the profoundness of the sleep, yet somehow the Americans took this vital cultural institution away. Our Mexican culture has been stripped of its normality.

On days when I am home, I get sleepy around one or two in the afternoon and fall into a trance that only a bed, my bright red Saltillo cobija, my sweaty pillow, and three Chihuahuas can appease. Tixoc crawls in between my legs and takes comfort in the heat of my legs. Luna positions her big culo near my hips and snores away while Xochitl sometimes settles near my shoulder or sometimes on top of my blanket on Tixoc who seems to care little about his woman cushioning herself on him. My Pekinese sleeps alone on his pillow. Next thing I know, my eyes shut themselves forcefully and I am gone. I do not know where I travel to; I just know I feel fantastic and rejuvenated; after a siesta, I have a second wind for the evening. Why can't we have siestas as part of our everyday life again?

I know I am not the only one who makes this point. High school kids who return from lunch cannot focus on the classroom because they are too sleepy. Teachers have told me that they cannot keep their attention, they just want the siesta they are deprived of. Maybe they would learn more if society was a little more compassionate, a nap will only help them out later in the day.

But no, this goddamn American society deprives us of our cultural attributes.

Las siestas must be reinstated, I feel too good after a nap in the afternoon.

Chapter Three

My Father's Construction Boots

When I was seven years old, I needed a pair of shoes. My feet were delicate, and I needed a pair of shoes. To Sears, my father and I went for my pair of shoes, excited, energized, thrilled, euphoric, and triumphant. A brand new pair of shoes, I could already smell the unused leather, the odorless inside and the shinning color not faded by wear and tear.

Mi papa me llevo because my mother was away attending to her ill father in Mexicali. For today, my father was mother too. My father and I entered Sears through the glass door in Inglewood and to the right were the pairs of shoes.

He directly went to the section of boots and selected a pair for me. I did not have a choice. My father smiled when they brought out my size. As I glanced at the pair of boots, I instantly became depressed. *Esos, no, esos, no!*

I could not wear that pair of boots; I was not going to wear those boots.

"Mira estan buenos: no quiero esas botas."

But, I couldn't really tell him why I did not want those boots. The beige, ankle-high, leather boots with a thick, tan, rubber sole with stitches below the shoestrings and a shoe horse shape. The shoestrings were more like rope that weaved through circular metal holes to tightly grip the boot to the foot as a person to secure the shoe firmly.

Still, I did not want those boots.

Those very boots that mi papa wore daily for his manual labor job were now the ones chosen for me. I did not want those similar construction boots for me because I felt that I would be mistaken for someone who was going to work in manual labor. I did not want those boots, for I felt my future was being chosen for me, solely by me putting on those boots. I was destined to hard labor as if a castigo, a punishment for life. I did not want to start at age seven. What had I done?

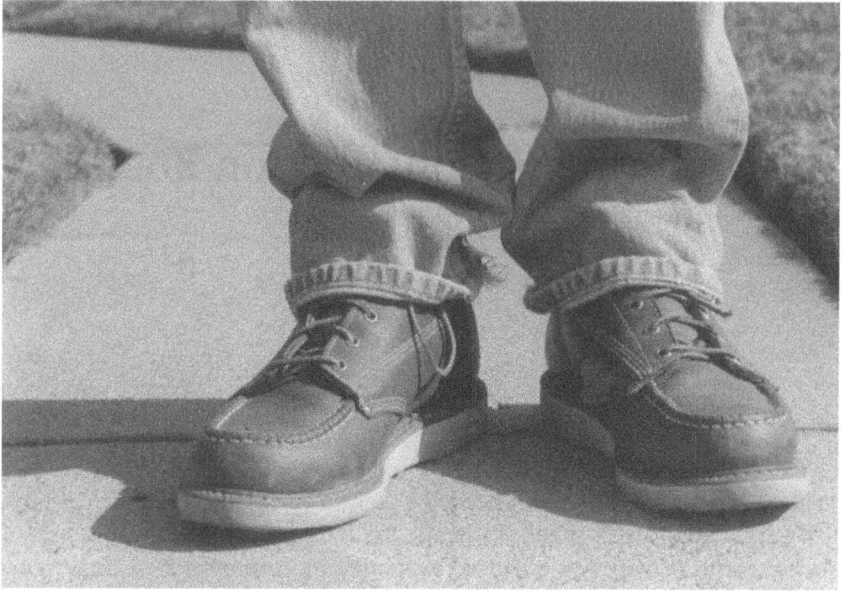

Figure 3.1. "Construction Boots"

The boots I had no choice but to wear them, and wear them to elementary school, I did. Those boots made me feel shame every time I stared down or in front of me as I walked. I felt they were walking me to a construction site instead of a classroom. It was as if those boots walked alone spiritually, fixated on my caste position to a life of manual American labor at minimum wage. I felt my future doomed by those boots.

I can still remember my father saying, "Estan buenos." For on that day, I needed a pair of boots, just like his.

Chapter Four

Basketball

My friend, Fernando, moved away in 1981 to south shores in San Pedro, somewhere to the south somewhere far away, distant from Inglewood. Prior to Fernando moving, his father, Kenny Hillman, explained the benefits of moving to me, Fernando, and another friend, Sammy. Closer to the beach. But we were close to the beach, we used to ride our bikes to Playa Del Rey. A swimming pool. A larger home where we could go and spend the weekends. It almost seemed as if the move was wrong for the right reasons and right for the wrong reasons. I sensed Kenny felt guilt for uprooting his son from his neighborhood and his comfort zone. I sensed a loss; we were once strangers now friends bonded by street football, street baseball, billiard sessions, hot-dog and hamburger events, even camping trips.

And just as we were promised, the Hillmans moved but kept their word. On a planned Friday, Sammy and I were picked up by Fernando's father; off to the back hills of San Pedro, we went. We had gone once before because we helped them move and rode on the back of the truck on the Harbor Freeway heading south. Fernando had moved, but our friendship had not been lost.

After viewing the house, I thought maybe Kenny was correct in moving his family twenty-five miles away. The house sat on the edge of a terraced hill overlooking the Pacific Ocean with a clear view of Catalina Island on a sunny day. The house had four bedrooms, two living rooms, a modest kitchen, and a nice swimming pool. The house was two-story with identical dimensions on the top and the bottom. The bottom was not wider as in conventional homes plus the best part was the driveway. The driveway was wide enough for two cars, so we could play basketball.

Back in Inglewood, Fernando's small drive way had a basketball rim. We all played basketball, but I never really enjoyed the sport. I did not comprehend

Figure 4.1. "Basketball"

the logic; plus, I was always impatient about shooting the ball, I did not like the sport. Now Fernando's father, Kenny, he loved basketball. He would play with us. He might have been the best White guy from Inglewood to play basketball. I could see his intensity as he played against my friend Scott's older brother who was a tall fifteen year old. Kenny was 5'10" and was only 28 years old then; thus he was young enough to play with us and old enough to intimidate us. It did help that he was an officer for the Los Angeles Police Department. We admired Kenny much more than our very own fathers, and he treated us like his children. Kenny kept his word, and fortunately, there was a rim to play basketball because one on one or two on two was always thrilling.

Sammy and I enjoyed being guests. We were fed; we swam. By four in the afternoon, Fernando's parents were off visiting friends, and we were allowed to be adults. Fernando's parents told us they were going to be out for a couple of hours and for us to stay home. We were in paradise; we did not have to wonder off. So when they left half an hour later, Sammy got the basketball and started taking some shots outside. We were twelve. We were three boys who had played street football and street basketball; we cheered, teased, and competed. Fernando would shoot the basketball, missing some and making some, Sammy always seemed to make the baskets, and I aimed aimlessly. I hated playing but enjoyed the camaraderie.

As we kept taking shots and cheering and howling as soon to be teenage boys do, a tall burly white man in shorts with graying hair and a beard walked across the street diagonally from the house in the corner towards us. As he neared, he called our attention, and we stopped making raucous.

As he approached us, he told us sternly: "Listen, you guys are making too much noise. You are interrupting my family's dinner in that corner room. You need to stop making so much noise. We want peace and quietness."

I was the closest to him and noticed his annoyance. His attitude intimidated me, and I froze as did Sammy and Fernando. We did not bounce the ball anymore.

Then the man stated: "If you don't stop making noise, I am going to call the cops."

He walked his fat ass away, across the street and into his house and up to his dining room. We stopped playing basketball, we were scared. We went inside the house.

The following morning, when we were having breakfast, we told Kenny how the man told us to be quiet and to stop playing basketball or he would have called the police on us.

We hoped for a protective response, but Kenny surprised us by saying: "If he had called the cops, I would have spanked you boys. You are not to make trouble."

I kind of got scared, not because my mother had given him the right to discipline me with a belt, but because he made me feel as if I—we—were wrong. We were just acting like kids, playing basketball. Kenny made me feel that the man was in his right to walk across the street and scold us for playing basketball and acting normal. Kenny had never told us back in Inglewood that we made too much noise.

I lost a sense of security and wondered about this new place where Fernando lived. Sure, the streets looked beautiful, the homes were gorgeous, you could see the Pacific Ocean from the living room, but we could not play basketball confidently. In Inglewood where Sammy and I still lived, nobody ever told us we could not play on the street because we made too much noise.

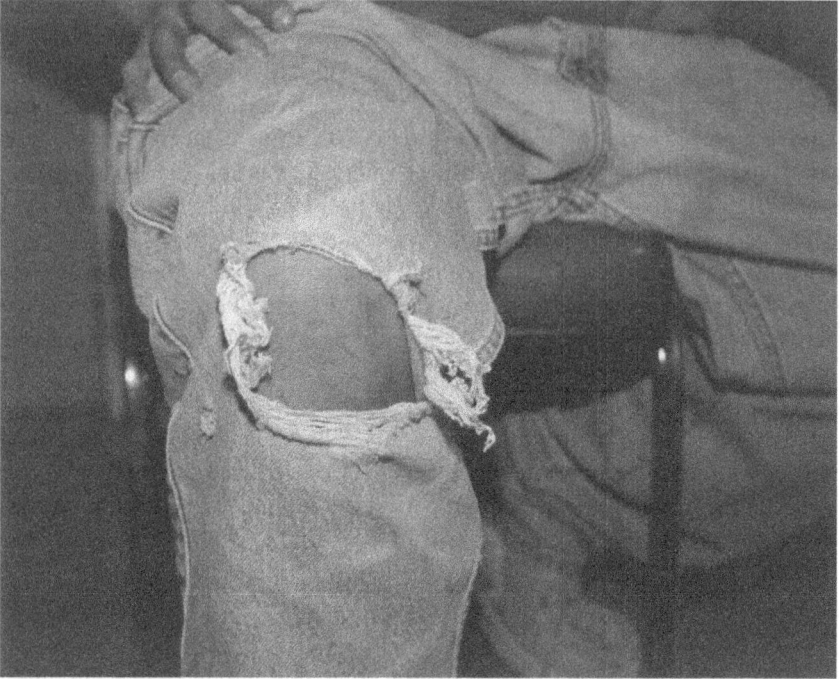

Figure 5.1. "Jeans with a Hole"

Chapter Five

The Coca Cola Patch

I was in my sophomore year of high school in 1985. My insecurity surrounded me like an ocean. I lacked confidence for many reasons. I lived in Inglewood two cities over, no females cariacias, I was not popular, only those who sat next to me knew I even existed, and I only had two pairs of pants, my Levi's.

My Levi's denim jeans were a carry over from two years prior before I exploded in weight, which was why I could wear those pants for close to three years. I had bought them from a weekend job I had cutting grass with a circular blade push lawnmower. That lawnmower was a relic from the 1940s and so was that home in Inglewood on Eucalyptus. We had lived there prior and the owner liked me, so he gave me this job at $20 a month, twice a month.

I earned every dollar on that mowing job because the handle broke and the man never fixed it. Hence, I would have to push the mower by the splintered wood, and by the end of two hours, I had blisters on my hands and my back ached. But, I bought my jeans.

And I wore them and wore them and wore them and wore them out.

At that time, I only had two pair of pants. Those years were extremely lean years in the height of Reagonomics, unemployment went up and down, and so did my mother's jobs. Our security was social security, our inheritance and life insurance policy from our deceased father, which paid for our rent and half of the food.

I remember the cost of living going up in 1984 because my mother would mention how the increase in rent meant less for other goods. My mother worked at a machine shop to make this difference up. Thus, I had to make these pants last as much as I could because there were four younger brothers. I had been good at making clothes last. In eighth grade, I wore one pair of

shoes from September almost to April. I had to make them last; my Levi's followed the same trajectory.

And I wore them and wore them out.

I would wear one pair and wash them when I got home. I would wear the
clean pair the next day. I had shirts and sweaters for those cold Los Angeles
winters but not pants. Eventually from so much washing, the jeans went from
their indigo hue to blue to light blue to light, light blue and then to white. My
jeans were now white, and worse, the fiber began to separate at the knee. I
was ashamed to be wearing jeans that were disfigured, but I had no choice.

Then one day, I found a Coca-Cola patch in the house. I do not know where
it came from or who bought it, but this Coca Cola patch now had a purpose:
to bind the shredding material on my right knee. My mother sewed it on by
machine. I was embarrassed, but I comprehended my reality. I walked around
unfazed about my patch but aware of this recent wound. Soon though, I paid
no attention to my patch as I went about my business.

Sometime later, as I sat in a World Studies class, a guy next to me who
dressed much like those *New Wave* freaks of the 80s asked me how I had gotten my pants so white. He told me that he wished he could get his pants similar to mine and that the Coca Cola patch was cool too. The guy's name was
Rahan, an Indian who dressed like a White guy from London. He would spike
his hair and wear checkered pants and pointy two-inch rubber sole shoes. I do
remember him wearing a jacket with patches from punk bands such as The
Dead Kennedys and The Sex Pistols. Those bands were as foreign as America itself to me. I was on survival mode; they were on a musical fad.

Internally, I laughed when this fashion-setter at Hawthorne High asked me
about my clothing. I wore my jeans daily because I had no choice, I used a
Coca-Cola patch to preserve one pair, and this guy thought my jeans were
great because of the color I was able to get them in. Without knowing, I might
have been a trend-setter due to my inability to purchase a new pair of pants.

I would have preferred a new pair of Levi's. I would have preferred a
kinder version of Reaganomics. Or better yet a society not so suicidal.

Chapter Six

The Bedroom

I would awake at 6:30 AM for high school from 1985 to 1989. For some reason in those days, waking up so early did not seem difficult. I would push myself up from the twin size bed I would sleep in. Sometimes, David's roaring snore would assist me in opening my eyelids. David, my younger brother, snored like a man, and like a man he handled the airborne pillows aimed at his face. Pillows would hit him right in the face, albeit gently. He would wake up frightened or talk in his sleep, *Estoppp*! Regardless of his reaction, he understood to turn to his side. By the morning, his snore did me a favor, and thus I pushed up and saw David and Ricardo asleep in two other beds. Somehow, we could fit three twin size beds into a twelve by eight foot room. During the day, the third bed hid under a higher than usual twin bed.

Nobody really had a bed though. Sometimes, I slept on the pullout bed as I was the last one to go to sleep or get home. My brothers were 10 and 11 years of age, and they were forced to sleep on schedule by my mother. She needed her peace too.

Before I went to sleep, I would go to the restroom, deposit my wastes, shower and then return to the hallway closet where my whole life seemed to fit. The closet was in between the bedroom and the bathroom. There in that closet of two doors was where I had my clothes, my shoes, and my extras. Some books, notebooks, letters from friends, junk that amounted to nothing yet made me believe I had privacy. My mother understood that I needed my space even if it was a hole closet. She forbade any of my brothers to tamper with it too.

I would wear the endless Levi jeans, tennis shoes, huaraches, a sweater or a light jacket, and off I went. But before I walked out, I would have a taco de chorizo con papas, always a glass of milk, pan dulce if I was lucky and a *buen*

Figure 6.1. "Garage Bedroom"

dia smile from my mother. I walked out to the depression of Lennox, the slum that entrapped me, turned left from the black metal door, navigated through the parked cars, zig-zagging, and walked onto the driveway out towards 106th Street. Ten feet north was the duplex house next to us, a similar metal door, bar windows, a flower bed where only weeds grew and then two garage doors. The garage doors were both brown from recent cosmetic paint jobs that seemed to hide the grime but never quite made those houses seem appealing.

Always, the first garage door was partially open; always I stared. There I saw a bed on top of a circular throw rug. There was a night table next to it with a lamp and a cross. The cross partially hung and right below a picture of the Virgen de Guadalupe. There was a light bulb hanging from the center of the garage. The inside of the garage was skeletal. The black tar paper was the background.

I always stared in the garage. I really couldn't help it; the garage bedroom was inside my visual periphery. I always saw this young guy, maybe in his early 20's sitting up on the edge of the bed but never wanting to stand up. As I walked, I saw his half closed eyes, wearing a white tank shirt and some gray sweats, rubbing the sleep off. He struggled to get up. He did not want to get up.

I always wondered how he went to the restroom. Did the neighbor leave the black metal door unlocked? Was she not afraid of strangers breaking in? Was she not afraid of Tepa at night whom socialized into the dawn? Did he urinate on the side of the house right next to ours where the clothesline was? The clothesline was not ours; we shared it, and on many occasions, I had some clothes missing, especially my shorts. Come to think, the clothesline area usually reeked with urine. My mother would wash with Clorox constantly.

Where did that young man ex-lax himself? How did he eat? I always noticed that the garage had many blankets during the winter, but during the summer how did he survive the suffocation from the lack of insulation? No breeze during those hot August nights. I doubt any fan would have sufficed. What about romance? Was the car the space or there too? I would stare and see this young Mexicano struggle to get up, struggle to face the routine, languish to feel hope that his jale would provide him with a real apartment, or just fight to survive in this "land of progress."

Every time I walked off to school and saw that young man in his garage, I thought to myself: how blessed I was to sleep on the floor inside a shack only ten feet away from a man sleeping in a garage.

I awoke to my nightmare every morning in an insulated room.

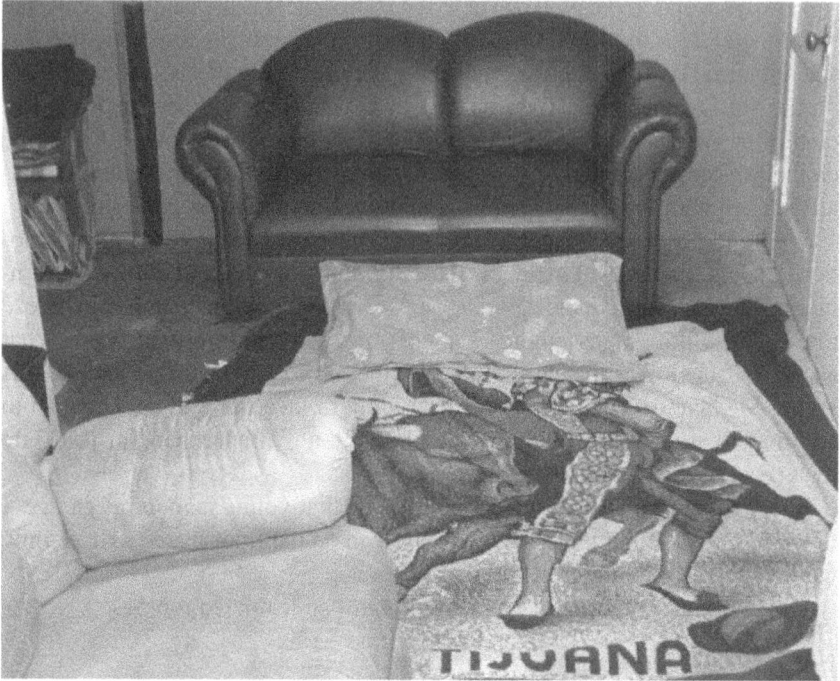

Figure 7.1. "Roommates"

Chapter Seven

Roommates

Although I believe that I am not suppose to have gripes about my mother at least not long lasting ones, I do have one: Throughout my life, I have always had animosity toward my mother because of our living arrangements growing up. My mother often had somebody living with us. I do not know the rational, but I comprehend the reason, economic survival. Social capital as some may say but at family social expense. Maybe my mother is unwise, but the result of her actions has been profound.

My early memory of this behavior is 1979; my mother met a lady in need at the laundrymat and had her stay at the house. Eventually, the lady and her child overstayed their visit, and if not for my mother acting firmly, the lady was ready to move in and leave the rest of us without a place to live.

It is hard to rationalize and comprehend the thinking. Without doubt, my mother carried a sense of obligation, for she was once in a similar situation. She had once stayed temporarily with her Tía Ester in Inglewood 1964 and later again in 1969 before she settled in with employment and a house of her own. Familial, societal, human compassion are all valid reasons, but my mother never had a sense of "no," irregardless of her family expanding. The madness continued as part of my upbringing.

After the laundrymat lady, my mother had a cousin of hers live with us from 1980 to 1981. The house was small, one bedroom. Who knows why she brought a roommate in? Maybe she felt overwhelmed being widowed just the year prior. Her cousin eventually returned to Mexicali after her father forbade her from romancing a man ten years her senior.

Two years later, my mother's madness resulted in the family relocating to Riverside for a "better life" only to share a home that had dirty carpet. The owner of the house, a Colombian Santero, lived in the converted garage and the den. We had the rest of the house, but we shared the kitchen and one rest-room. I hated that life. I roamed Magnolia Avenue hoping to be lost, but I never attempted to run away because I knew the streets were worse. I had to aguantarme, suffer this chingada American life.

Six months later, we returned to Inglewood, my hometown. Out in River-side, I had my first encounter with marijuana with some White trash heavy metal listeners who only knew about Inglewood from their visits to the Fo-rum and some third generation Mexicans who fit the American sociological description of them, drunks, junior high dropouts, collecting cans for money who somehow provided enough love to me by giving me the proceeds. The older English speaking Mexicano, Lauren, might have drank Budweiser, but he took an interest in me.

Not even a year later in 1984, my mother moved another roommate into the house, a lady and her son to share the bills. There was no consultation, no wondering how this would affect us, my mother just acted as the owner of our space. We were comfortable, there were two sets of bunk beds and two bed-rooms. We lived comfortably for a few months. Once Guillermina and her son (the new roommates) arrived, I was shipped out to the plastic sofa in the liv-ing room. I hated my mother with a passion for this. Sometime later, there was fallout with Guillermina and the landlord, for having two extra people living in the rental. My mother should not have jeopardized our living arrangement because housing discrimination against Mexicans was rampant. Few White landlords would rent to large families, and my mother by trying to save on partial rent got us expelled.

Nevertheless, this decision was not to solely be blamed on her. Reaganomics was at its peak, and everybody was suffering worse than the Jimmy Carter era of gas rationing. Now people were home-rationing, and I was being put out on a plastic sofa which made me perspire the whole night and dehydrated me spiritually.

I hated this life, suicidal tendencies circulated in my head.

Due to my mother's ill-conceived survival tactic, we were forced to move to another place that turned out to be the worse neighborhood we had ever lived in. Indirectly, I have never forgiven her for that.

Our next place was in Lennox where I hid. Three years later, we had an-other roommate, my mother's brother in law. He had moved up from Mexi-cali to stay for two months in order to save some money; however, he ended up staying for two years. He did not pay rent until I told him to do so, which was toward the end of the second year. My mother failed to be assertive and charge him rent, and even worse, she would not back me up when I said something. She was quick to scold me but not fast enough to defend our pri-vate space, which was no longer private. We lived in a two-bedroom chicken coop, one bedroom for her and my youngest brother and the second room for the other four of us. The living room was shot. That husband of my mother's sister laid out his two blankets and slept on the floor.

I had no problem with the two-month stay, but he wore out his welcome, he failed to pay enough rent. On top of that, he gambled most of his money away—that was why he had to stay, he was irresponsible; he Vegased his money away instead of finding a place of his own. Illegality was not an issue, he had residency and worked as a carpenter.

Only my emotional outburst made him leave. I could not comprehend him not recognizing the animosity we had toward him. All he did was provide a sad face, make me feel guilty and laugh behind our backs as he lived rent free. And my mother would not take a stand. I hid away in college and my girl-friend's house, I felt homeless. I only showed up to sleep and left as early as possible.

Half way through the leech's stay, another roommate arrived. My cousin Victor (the son of my other Tía Beva) arrived. Now the living room was more of a third bedroom. I tried to be friendly, cordial, and helpful with employ-ment prospects, but I despised this life. From him, I learned how poverty wears on Mexicans, as Mexican companies charging fees to help Mexicans find employment were merely swindlers exploiting the cultural connection. Even Victor lost it once and physically hit my second to youngest brother, David. I yelled at him, and the days of him staying there ended soon after. Eventually, my cousin left to Bell Gardens and then later followed the mi-gratory trail to New York, where he lost his work permit in the early 1990s because the INS refused to renew it. He was not needed anymore.

If anyone states that Mexicans do not assist each other, my upbringing proves just the opposite. What is further proven is that this kind of aid can erode family unity. The American social structure strains those here for its profit, and in return we fight amongst ourselves, even against our mothers be-cause they may be driven by guilt to aid.

Later, another roommate showed up. This time, the son of my uncle, an-other headache, another dilemma, another problem. And if up to my mother, she would have his mother come live with her too, but the space did not per-mit her to do so.

Even as we got older and more financially stable, my mother continued her aid-to-relatives madness. In 1999, I bought a duplex so my mother and younger brother would not have to worry about renting and rent increases. However, instead of cherishing the 3-bedroom space in a nice, safe neigh-borhood, my mother followed her old pattern. She allowed friends to park cars on the driveway as a sort of storage facility, she allowed my cousin Es-teben to move in again, and eventually, she allowed her boyfriend to move in with her. Not once did she ask me—her son, the landlord—if it was alright. She continued to be ruled by guilt. When I made them move up to the smaller, 2-bedroom unit so that I could move on with my life and have a bigger space for my dogs, she and my brother got very upset. Where would my cousin go? They worried about a 26-year-old man who earned $15 per hour.

The tragedy is that my brother now lives with this mindset and believes I am at fault for wanting privacy. Unfortunately, my mother and brother have gotten permanently entangled and have no notion of how to live alone—they are now making me suicidal. Suicidal not in the definition of actually dying but in the permanent spiritual death of us, as a unit of what was once a family.

Throughout all of these experiences, what I could never understand was why endanger our living space, why make the children uncomfortable, why disrespect family boundaries? My resulting anger has driven me to prefer isolation, a hermit-like lifestyle where I am secluded from uninvited guests.

Maybe my nino was correct: when my father asked him why he had plastic milk crates in his living room instead of a sofa, my nino Gus, responded, "So when people come and visit, their ass will hurt and they will not overstay." They laughed away at the reality.

Chapter Eight

Louie's White Monte Carlo

Louie was unlike any of the high schoolers I knew. He had a great smile, fair skin (yes, Mexicans have fair skin) and chino or wavy hair. Louie and I were on the wrestling team. He was tall, around 5'11 and flaco. But Louie was a hustler, not in the pimping sense, rather in the Mexican sense: Louie worked hard. He practiced the hardest, for in wrestling, a six-minute match is an eternity. During practice, the wrestling room became a sauna, after much rolling around in endless perfections and repetitions of body moves that would help us win medals or at least not get pinned.

I joined the wrestling team because I enjoyed the one on one competition. I needed this for my self-esteem. If I lost, I lost; if I won, I won all by myself. Not overlooked and not under looked. Participating in this sport was a sacrifice because I got out of school around five in the evening, more exhausted than ever. Tired or not, I had to walk north to the dungeons of Lennox.

Lennox was the armpit of the South Bay, the South Bay did not want to claim Lennox, but there we were under the path of the arriving airplanes, with the same ocean breeze as Manhattan Beach or Torrance. Walking to high school was a bitch because it was outside the community. Hawthorne High School was the next city over to the south; Lennox was unincorporated county that belonged to the County of Los Angeles. Nobody wanted us; we were city-less, as if we did not exist. We only belonged to the county because nobody else would claim us.

Getting to the high school was a challenge because Hawthorne High was three miles south and one mile west. The school district did not provide a bus. Transportation was in itself a struggle. Extra curricular activities had to be thought out. Can I get there on time if my mother is working? Will it be too late?

It seemed as if they wanted us to drop out and not attend.

Figure 8.1. "Monte Carlo"

Eventually, I got used to walking or taking the bus. Us Lennox kids had to go to Boy's Market and buy our limousine-bus pass for $5 dollars a month. And every month I did. I wrestled and walked, which added to my conditioning since I would walk one mile east on Broadway to Hawthorne Boulevard and wait in front of the Hawthorne Mall. After a while, I learned that by 5 PM, the frequency of the RTD was reduced. I then began to walk directly north up Inglewood Avenue and eventually crossed east into Lennox. All tired out. It seemed I walked faster than the bus drove north. Waiting for the number 40 bus drove me insane; minute by minute, I gave up on the RTD. I would rather walk; I had been taught to fly as fast as I could on my feet.

In wrestling, I struggled, rarely won but never gave up. I started to wrestle during my sophomore year; I wanted to be part of high school beyond a student, regardless of the distance from my home.

Louie was one of the better wrestlers who had improved from the beginning of the season, who practiced the hardest and who never complained even though many of us gasped for air and water. As a result, Louie's wrestling skills improved that year, his senior year. After wrestling season, he began to work. By the beginning of the next school year, Louie bought himself a long, red, used Monte Carlo. The Monte Carlo was long, like a boat, but Louie had a car. He was moving up in life even though he lived in Hawthorne's north east corner across from Lennox.

I worked diligently at wrestling but progressed little; in fact, I lost more matches than I won. Just as I set into my ritual—my long journey home—something changed: Louie would offer me a ride to Hawthorne Boulevard. This ride was bliss, this ride would cut my walk by three miles.

As soon as he offered the ride, I jumped in. Leaning back, cruising Mexican style yet serious, Louie drove. The red velvet driver's seat tilted back from the many years of use, but Louie drove steadily with his right hand resting on the top of the steering wheel. During the ride, he was mostly quiet as his exhaustion peeped through. Sometimes, he would drop me off at Hawthorne Boulevard. Other times, he would drive me all the way to 106th Street in Lennox. He did so with great concern and as frequently as he could. He gave me enough rides for me to feel embarrassed to accept his offer as if I was a burden. And yet, I could never say no, because the thought of walking was to be *bien jodido*.

Months later, Louie had the Monte Carlo painted white. I was in a new vehicle being chauffeured home by an older kid. It was one kid caring for another kid when the school district should have provided that support. He seemed to also be concerned about my safety. For when people heard Lennox mentioned, they cringed.

Every time Louie dropped me off, I said thanks but knew deep in my heart I could never repay him. As he would drive off, I would stare at the white Monte Carlo as it headed east towards Prairie Boulevard and realized he cared for me as human beings should care for one another.

I will always remember Louie and the white Monte Carlo because that used car sheltered me as a teenager wrestling with life in a greater community that did not want me or any of the children in Lennox. They did not provide busing even though we Lennox kids were in the district and did not live in the city of Hawthorne.

I still see that White Monte Carlo driving away. My school bus was white, not yellow.

Figure 9.1. "Homes"

Chapter Nine

My Mother Will Never Own a Home

There are two profound scars in my soul, psychic, espiritu, anima, memory and everyday life that continue to shape my mere existence. The first one is the death of my father at age eleven—a death which occurred by nature, out of the control of anybody, any God, any dog, any prayer. The only god, *death,* arrived and took my father. His time was up. I learned to live with that fact; I have seen his tomb for more years (24 years exactly) than my eleven years of life with him.

Seeing how my mother would drive by beautiful homes in Manhattan *Bitch* and San Pedro, stare at them, and appreciate with some envy continues to eat at my soul with a vengeance, vengeance toward the Americanization of society, the notion of property ownership, the exclusivity of property ownership and all of its benefits. I believe only death will soothe my anger, but even then death will not forget my ineptness at my mother's longing, for I have penned this animosity for eternity. My mother wanted a beautiful home, not a mansion just a tract home with a garage and the comforts all those Gringos had in their homes.

My mother would drive bye in our red station wagon and just stare covering her eyes from the glare of the sun. She stared not with envy but with admiration as was noted in her tone, "Que hermosura." I would look down and realize my mother would never own a home like those fancy cardboard shacks and neither would I. She dreamed, I nightmared.

And just like the death of my father, I too am scarred by the meanness in this society. For my mother is a prime example of how hard work does not correlate to progress. My mother has worked the hardest of anybody I have ever known. She raised five boys as a widowed woman in the Reagan years and has worked in every conceivable job in Los Angeles. She has worked as a maid, seamstress, curtain-maker, food preparer, airline food preparer, a beautician, early childhood educator others would call babysitter. She has sold Mary Kay, Avon, and Tupperware. She has worked in a dish factory, a furniture factory, a metal machine shop, and a baseball cap factory. And her most important job was being a mother. Not one of these vital jobs positions compensated her adequately either. They were minimum wage jobs that made somebody else rich. My mother was the perfect slave who paid taxes, both federal and state, yet was never allowed to amount to anything, much less to owning a home.

She would purposely drive to Manhattan Bitch or Torrance, pretend to shop and afterwards slowly drive around neighborhoods admiring somebody else's beautiful home. She would later say: "Nombre, por eso me voy para salirme de este chiquero, Lennox, y no regreso hasta la noche cuando ha oscurecido y no se ve tan feo."

My mother would leave the chicken coop as she called Lennox and would not return until after darkness set in. The obscurity would hide the grime of Lennox. She would tell me about Lomita, Palos Verdes, Redondo Bitch and how even the Pic'N'Save had better quality and better deals: "No venden yonke alli."

I, however, did not appreciate those homes. Why did I not live in a similar home with enough bedrooms, with a small backyard and front yard, with no car blocking the entrance or no car blowing exhaust into the living room as us kids watched television? I could not hope as my mother did, I could only vent—vent at this suicidal society that kept us poor.

As a teenager, I began to see how unfair this society was. I befriended some white kids at this crazy, superstitious born-again church. To be honest, I felt like a hypocrite because I went along with, what I as a Native American call their paganism and lies, so I could view their better homes, the kind everybody should have. Then, one day I quit going; I was not going to be tormented by my own guilt or fooled by my façade. I never believed as much as I lied myself into believing their superstition. Why would I want to go to their heaven? Wasn't one life time enough of a difference?

Moreover, I hated them because they knew they benefited from being White, and I was disadvantaged for being Mexican. I even once pretended to not speak Spanish, but I was pretending in order to not be left out. I really hated them because my mother worked all her life, yet most of these people did not. Many of them had inherited money, bought homes, and gained equity. My mother worked all her life and had not amounted to anything. She would have been better off on welfare versus slaving for minimum wage from some fucking Korean or some fucking Mexican who was the front exploiter for a fucking American.

I really hated every white neighborhood in the South Bay because they had more and had done the least amount to get it. They didn't work harder than any Mexican I knew because they did not work the dirtiest or lowest paying jobs. And yet Whites lived in the nicest neighborhoods, with large homes where they all could fit comfortably. We, for all intended purposes, lived like sardines.

And still my mother drove into those neighborhoods to escape just like I did. She could only view them driving by slowly and that was as close as she got. I tried to ignore those places but really couldn't. Our high school was in a better neighborhood than Lennox, the supermarkets were cleaner outside of Lennox, shopping for clothes at the South Bay Galleria was better than Lennox, parks in El Segundo and Torrance were safer than Lennox Park, streets were cleaner, movie theaters were outside of Lennox, our work was outside of Lennox. Everything was better outside of Lennox except us Mexicans. I pretended to not see the better neighborhoods, but I was only lying to myself.

I hated life, them, and America. I knew my mother would never own a home in America, the land of the free White people.

Figure 10.1. "Football Jersey and Helmet"

Chapter Ten

Why My Brother Was Never Drafted

When I was a child, Saturdays were days I looked forward to. I would wake up early, 7 AM with no hesitation. I ran to the living room a whole eight steps and would turn on the black and white television. I forgot about the restroom or the corn flakes until my emotion was calmed by the first program. Cartoons were a Saturday addiction; I watched them on ABC until 9 or 11 AM at which time the cartoons were replaced by another set of funnies: college football.

At first, I hated the interruption, but then I got used to it. I especially liked it when my father would sit and watch games. My father loved football. Although he would only watch part of the games, he followed the plays consistently. I, on the other, did not understand the game very well, but after a while, through him, I came to enjoy the game. I remember when the Rams made the 1979 Superbowl, and I mentioned to my father that the Rams were going to win. He just laughed and said, "No mijo, van a ganar los esteelers." And true to the prediction, the Rams lost. When he arrived home from his favorite sport, horse racing, he told me, "Que te dije, que iban a ganar los Steelers."

My father knew football well, and why would he not; he was born and raised in southern California were football was popular even for Spanish-speaking folks. In fact, the most crowded high school football game west of the Mississippi is not in Texas but in East Los Angeles: The Mexican capital of the Mexican capital in the United States . The East Los Angeles Classic between Roosevelt High School and Garfield High School, simply known as The Classic, is where the cheerleaders dance to cumbias and norteñas as part of their routines and 25,000 fans taunt and cheer each other on, as if they were in some pueblo. And they are, we just call it East Los Angeles.

Mexicans in the U.S. love football, and my father proved that. My mother has told me that he wished one of his sons played football. He hoped that one

31

of his sons would play on television for one of those universities, while he attended college. He knew he could never attend, but maybe one of us would.

And football I played when I got to high school. But I realized it was harder than it appeared. I was not aggressive enough nor had I been exposed to the physicality of the game nor had I been in shape for the game. I was a tall clumsy sophomore who could barely run. I had not played football before high school because I was not exposed to the bureaucracy, where would I sign up at, where would I play, and how would I pay for it. Every extra dollar was vital after the breadwinner died. I had tried baseball three years earlier, but I was such an awful player, my friends on the opposing teams wished I would get a hit. I dropped pop-flies and direct hits to right field; the Black coaches could not scold me anymore. I refused to play the following year out of embarrassment and gave up on baseball long before that.

But I got an itch in 9th grade from hearing players talk about the game the day before. Hearing them instilled in me a desire to play futbol americano. So in the spring of 1984, I saw the announcements and went to try out. I was told to get cleats, which I did from Big Five, but when I put them on, all the Black players began to laugh from their waists up almost falling off to their sides because I was using Black Puma soccer cleats instead of white football cleats. I did not know the difference, a shoe is a shoe.

"Hey Camacho, you gonna play soccer out here, jajajajajajajajaja."

"Look at him with his black Puma soccer cleats."

I was the only player out of 45 athletes who wore black cleats. I stood out too. That was how foreign futbol Americano was for me that I could not tell the difference in their style of cleats. Oddly enough, I stopped playing soccer after my elementary years during which time we would play on a huge field, and all we had to do was chase the ball through the dust and try to kick it against our opponents. Even then, we played with our tennis shoes not with cleats. We were not that serious.

Although the Black players laughed their Black asses off, from today's football standards I might have been considered a pioneer. I do not want to take athletic fashion credit though, but I was one of the first to wear black cleats for football uniforms in 1985. Nowadays, most football cleats are black.

And football I learned to play after much practice from two years of training. I was a sidelined participant; I watched the game through my helmet and played when the other team had been decisively defeated. But my senior year, I did well enough to start. I had gotten stronger and smarter; I understood the techniques and played right offensive tackle. There were Mexicans on the team, but I was the only one who started among the Black, White, and Samoan players.

Overall, as an athlete, I came into fruition my senior year. I was a success because I had different people from work who attended my game and supported me. My wrestling coach's father, Mr. John Bree Sr., made positive comments about my playing. Mr. Bree was our team photographer (but once a wrestling coach himself who qualified wrestlers for the state tournament).

Mr. Bree Sr. said to me once, "Hey, Camacho, you've been doing very good out there on the field, seems like you might be all league."

Those words gave me more confidence than anything else. Mr. Bree Sr. was an amiable person. I always enjoyed his company during the wrestling tournaments, so his words were highly esteemed by me.

Some days later during lunch at Jim's Charbroiled hamburgers in Lennox with my wrestling coach, John Bree Jr., I mentioned to him about possibly making the all star league team.

"I do not think so."

"Why?" I asked him perplexed.

"It's because the all star teams are chosen during a meeting with all the coaches and they are not going to pick you. You don't fit their description," he explained.

I did not quite comprehend though I suspected there was a problem with the coaches. Coach Bree was being honest with me first and foremost because we were buddies. He was my teacher in many ways. And true to the point, I was not chosen for any award from the league coaches, not even an honorable mention. Yet, the athletes that were chosen from Hawthorne were athletes who I blocked quite easily.

One winner was the defensive end, a tall Armenian, who I enjoyed playing against because he was lanky. His center of gravity was quite high, so I did not have to get low with him. I would rush him like a bull and move him two yards back.

The other winner was a stocky Black midget who played defensive tackle. He was low, but I learned to lower my body from my wrestling seasons and blocking him was easy.

In the end, John Bree Jr. was correct. I was not going to be chosen because I did not fit the mold of those white coaches. The name, the skin, the neighborhood, the background had all been hindrances for me even though I did not play organized football until age fifteen.

What can you do about stereotypes? I tried to play junior college football, progressed well as a second stringer, but I lost patience and wanted to see the world. After one year, two summers and my first love, I focused solely on school and went to Bolivia. Football or Bolivia? I began to see the world, but I had planted a seed.

A few years later, my brothers started to play. Alberto (my brother next in line) was a better athlete, but his temper and recklessness distracted him. He started as a freshman, but by his senior year had quit. Although he started all three years, the Camacho legacy at Hawthorne High School came from Ricardo and David. David was the taller one who was 6'3" at age fourteen. Before, I was the tall one at 6'3" only to lose my uniqueness to David who sprang up to 6'7" by his senior year. Ricardo was no slouch, but he remained at 6'2". Our height comes from our mother's blood. Mexican Apaches from the north are tall and we were the tallest.

By the end of their high school careers, they had played in 28 varsity games in two years, ten games per season plus playoffs. My brothers' team made it to back to back divisional championships. Their junior year they won. Their senior year they lost though they were the better team, statistics and so forth.

When it came time for awards, my brother, David, received no recognition, yet he was a man among boys. Black and White athletes had articles written about them for their individual talents yet not David. The year prior an Egyptian player on the team was given all kinds of newspaper recognitions, but the offensive line coach stated, "I don't understand why Mustapha got so much attention, he wasn't that good."

Ricardo would tell me, "You should have seen the way David beat the shit out of all those players."

I noticed that the rival, Palos Verdes Peninsula High School, the Green Sticks got most of the recognition. Even the local newspaper, *The Daily Breeze*, a suburban low IQ, right-wing paper would do comparative stories where the pictures of the all White boy offensive line was shown smiling in a bigger picture on top, while the all Mexican offensive line from Hawthorne High was pictured in a smaller size print with their helmets on. Pictures say a thousand words. When I mentioned what I saw to the old-timer coach, Otto Plum, he replied, "What do you expect from the Daily Breeze?" Not much. My brothers' team beat the shit out of Peninsula High both years.

And yet I saw the same racist treatment toward David.

David was given All First Team League Award and so was Ricardo but on the Second Team All League. Even though they were back to back division finalists, David was not awarded as the best lineman. I questioned the representative from the L.A. Times, and all he stated was the other player John Wellborn (whose father was an attorney) had played both ways. I told him that at Hawthorne High, few players went both ways. They tried to play as many as possible, plus David had manhandled Wellborn in their rival game. David was the key blocker.

I was livid; David had earned that recognition as the best lineman on merit. When a person works hard, all he expects is his just compensation. But David was not recognized and did not even earn a scholarship because he was missing one science laboratory class. Nobody paid attention to him.

After graduation, Ricardo and David played junior college football at Harbor College where they were relegated to crowds of twenty-five people, primarily parents. Both Ricardo and David excelled at Harbor. David was chosen all conference but was awarded honorable mention on the All-American team.

By then, I worked at Compton College where the football coach, Art Perkins (who had played for the Los Angeles Rams in the early 1970s as a fullback), mentioned that he thought my brother should have made First Team All American not Honorable Mention.

The key difference was in recruitment. This made a difference between one major university over another, between a University of California and a California State University. Art even mentioned that my other brother Ricardo was the bigger surprise because he played on the blind spot and had done an exceptional job in blocking the quarterback.

Recognitions and titles mean something in America, America knows that well. Their hierarchies in colleges could be the difference in admission to graduate school; their graduate schools could be the difference in employment; their law schools mean the difference in salaries. America knows what I am saying.

I had become the father of my brothers when I was ten years old. I was told by my crying uncle in 1980 that since my father had passed away, I was the man of the house. I would have to watch out for my little brothers, for nobody else would. Watching out was what I had been doing since I was a teenager, paving the road was my duty. My brother Alberto once said, "None of us joined the military because you didn't." I was counseling my brothers in the same way that white folks send their kids to SAT training or football camps. I was their college counselor because my counselor at El Camino College, one Armando Gonzales, was a worthless counselor who yelled at me because I had to work and did not take math in my first semester of college. I never returned to him again, I counseled myself and went to other white counselors for follow-ups. I was my own counselor in life, for I had no other counselor in the Gabacho world. I became my brother's counselor because the White world only counsels each other.

And true to form, David and Ricardo had problems again. The football coach told me at Harbor that USC was going to offer David a scholarship, but we never heard from them again. Not even a courtesy, "No, thank you, we have changed our minds." David was ignored by every school in California including lowly San José State. I put calls in for him and only when the lineman coach thought I could be of service to him by finding jobs for his San Jose State players did he show some interest. I ignored him after.

David was recruited by Memphis, Louisville, Utah and Oklahoma State. He chose Oklahoma State, but the worst part was they recruited him because the recruiter from Oklahoma State went to observe another player at Harbor College. When he saw David's playing and size, he approached him. Pure fluke.

My father's dream was realized—David went to Oklahoma State. However, Ricardo was ignored until he went to Northridge as a backup.

Overall, I was upset at the way my brothers were treated by USC and Northridge, so I wrote a letter of complaint. I received a nasty call from the USC line coach, although I do not know how he got my number. During the heated conversation, I told him that they should have had the respect to tell my brother they were not interested. I also told him that the Fresno State coach said to David that USC mentioned in their coaches' meetings that they had recruited him. The USC coach demanded the coach's name, but all I said was, "Go talk to them yourself and get some class in the future." I never heard from that White asshole again.

David went to Oklahoma State University in 1995. This was the best place for him to train and compete. He did well. He started for two years. He was the tallest player in college football. He had made my father's dream come true, but in the brochure, the university got his residency incorrect. They wrote Compton and not Lennox, though his high school was in Hawthorne. These places were twelve miles away from each other. Lennox was a barrio that was poorer than Compton but safer. Compton sounded too Black and Black it behaved. They believed Mexicans had invaded their Black America when this was once the Dominguez Rancho in the Mexican state of California.

Lennox did not receive recognition and neither did David. There was never a news story about a local kid, chavo, chico from Lennox who was succeeding in football at Oklahoma State University. Some articles predicted he would be drafted into the National Football League in the third round, and others said he was the greatest lineman at OSU. OSU, the same university that Hall of Famer, Barry Sanders, attended.

David played well in the Big Twelve conference too. We saw him on television when he played in the Alamo Bowl. He blocked well enough to make All Conference Second Teams twice against the likes of teams from Nebraska, Texas and Oklahoma. David even made the 1998 Hula Bowl College All Stars where he blocked for Ricky Williams; we have a great picture of him playing in Hawaii.

But David would tell me, "Toda la atencion se la dan a los negros y blancos." (All the attention is given to the Blacks and Whites.) David had high hopes, he was led to believe in them.

Ricardo opted to stay at Cal State University, Northridge where he was never given a probability. He was chosen as a backup and chastised for my complaint letter of his mistreatment during the recruitment period. His coach, Dave Baldwin, approached him with the letter and ignored him the whole year. Protecting your kin against these coaches can have negative ramifications. Ricardo later said he gave up on playing but still attended practice because he was on scholarship. He traveled and saw states such as Montana, Utah and New Mexico.

The next year, the coach left to San José State, but it only got worse. The new coach, Jim Fenwick (the former coach from Valley College), offered a bribe of one thousand dollars to Ricardo in exchange for him quitting the team and subsequently losing his scholarship. Ricardo was now a senior and had only seen his situation worsen with this new son of a bitch. Jim Fenwick was not even interested in the academic completion of my brother's education. When Ricardo said no, Fenwick retaliated by excluding him from the travel team. On the team's first travel game, they went to Hawaii and Ricardo was not taken. A direct humiliation to say the least.

Ricardo's offensive line coach, Aaron Gideon, knew it was wrong and so did many other players who stated to Ricardo that the actions of Fenwick were mean-spirited. Ricardo was a senior, the first backup on the offensive line the year before, and now he was not worthy of being on the travel team. I offered to write a letter to the NCAA about the bribe, but Ricardo stated he would prove Fenwick wrong. He stayed on, attended every practice, and completed the season. His line coach, Aaron Gideon, even commended his perseverance under such disrespect.

The problem with these fucking white coaches is that they act like goddamn generals, as if they were in some kind of army with no one to answer to even when what they are doing is morally wrong. This "general" would sacrifice one of his soldiers for his advancement. How can we ever trust White authority? I was angry at such treatment but admired Ricardo in proving that mother fucker coach wrong and for completing his studies in Chicano Studies. Ricardo had had an incredible run that ended bitterly, but life was now moving on. Memories of success were eighty percent good. College football was—and is—full of exploitations. The scholarship amounted to 24 cents per hour, according to Ricardo.

After Ricardo's fiasco, all hope was on David. As draft day neared, the whole family was excited. A rag to riches story a la mexicana. Draft day came and went to no avail. A la mexicana we stayed. He was not drafted even though he had a track record of proven efficiency in the Big 12 conference, the Hula Bowl, height at 6'7" and weight at 300 pounds. The man could bench press 400 pounds; he did not use steroids either. Disappointment, regret, lament, anger, disenchantment, frustration, disillusionment, bitterness, a fuck you to the false pretense of hard work were felt.

Here, merit mattered not a bit. He saw Black and White athletes that he blocked well against were given the green light of acceptance. He saw John Wellborn, a high school opponent, be drafted from Cal. Just like that any sense of accomplishment was ended. He would have accepted rejection if he was not up to par, but an athlete at this level knows his skill.

Some months later, he attended some Raiders' practices. Interestingly, the Raiders stated he scored low on his written exam. They were told he was dyslexic, but they would not budge. Still, it's hard to imagine that the man with Charles Manson's alter ego doesn't have illiteracy compassion for those Blacks and thugs who need a second chance. It is hard to believe that a literacy exam is used in the NFL; it seems like a convenient excuse.

Later, David was signed as a free agent by the Baltimore Ravens (the year they won the Super Bowl), but he was cut the second to the last squad. The line coach liked him, but the head coach had his mind made up.

David would tell me, "These guys have their minds made up on who has made the team, there is no chance here. If they want to develop some young person, they will nurture and protect him. The veterans tell you, easy rookie and you can never prove your point, unless you are Black and White. They like the Black guys because they believe they can be trained. They like the white guys because they think they are "smart." So they give them chances. They don't know what to do with a Mexican. Man, had I been Black or White I would be right there."

Some time after that, David played with the XFL in New York where he injured his knee. Next, he was then taken by the Canadian Football League in Toronto and British Columbia. Both times, he was released on the last day. These guys all think in the same stereotypical way: who can play, who cannot because of their race. To think that coaches are equal opportunity employers based on talent only, is perpetuating the most egregious example of racial stereotypes. They chose—and still choose—based on race.

One time, the former football coach at Roosevelt High School in East Los Angeles, José Casagran, said that rarely did college recruiters go and see Mexican kids play football. He also explained that only 22 players start and 50 others stand and watch the game. Were there not any spaces there for any Mexican football players who could get an education and watch the game along other Black and White players?

Even the Mexican coach at East Los Angeles College falls into the same racial stereotypes of exclusion. Prior to the program being reinstated, there were only a handful of Blacks on the campus. They could be counted on two hands. After one semester of football, there were many young Black males from Fremont or Manual Arts High School in central or south Los Angeles, fifteen miles away. Some of my Mexicans students would state, "Chale, with the favoritism, I quit."

Many would say this same thing, including my brother. David would say, "You know Julián, my Black or White coaches did not help me. I did everything on my own to the best of my ability. I had no support."

The few white men we knew were always making excuses why David was not drafted: he was not strong enough, a little out of shape. Yet, nobody listened to him, the ill treatment, neglect and denial.

Two years ago, John Wellborn (David's high school rival) signed a $25 million dollar contract with the Philadelphia Eagles while David with a Bachelor of Arts in History from Oklahoma State University was working for Sam's Club in Tulsa in the tire center for $10 an hour plus benefits for his family. During the 2005 NFL season, John Welbourn was suspended for steroid use by his new team, the Kansas City Chiefs.

My brother did not get drafted into the NFL, but this cheater—among others—did. In this suicidal society, it always pays to cheat.

Figure 11.1. "Birkenstocks"

Chapter Eleven

Birkenstocks are Fancy Huaraches

Ever since I can remember, I have worn huaraches. Mexican leather sandals with the leather crisscrossing and snuggling the feet. The soles were made of leather if authentic. I never wore huaraches with left over tire rubber soles. There was a status to wearing huaraches. If you wore the ones with tire soles and a partial uni or royal or fir (firestone) without the estone, that made you corriente. Corriente I was not, or so I believed.

Man, I wore my huaraches during high school with pride and shorts. After all, huaraches are the original sandals from Northern Mexico. Even so, my huaraches wearing days were soon to be over because my feet grew beyond the measurement of any Mexican I knew. During high school, I wore a size 13 and was 6 feet 3 inches tall. Fortunately though, I could find huaraches my size on trips to Mexicali. After a while, I noticed that I continued to grow and so did my feet; I wore a size 14 and was 6 feet 5 inches tall.

For the longest time, I was the tallest Mexican I had ever come across except for some uncles who were my same height. I was almost taller than most Blacks and Whites that I knew. Mexican Mayo Yakis of the north have always been known for their height. I was just a continuation.

I wore my huaraches when I did not work, lounged, or when the sun was strong. I wore them so much that the soles holed due to my dragging pace, an unintentional pace. And by the time I knew it, my two pairs of huaraches were no more.

When I was twenty three years old on a trip to San Felipe in the Golfo de California, I ran into a small one man shop. The man had a Sears black sewing machine, leather soles huaraches for sale. I was in bliss. First, I asked him the price, fourteen dollars. Then, I asked if he had my size. He said, Si! When I paid him for them with a twenty, I noticed that my change was only

$2. I asked him why he gave me less change, and he explained that those huaraches, size 14, cost $18.

I thought, *Ah cabron, I have to pay more for my physique which I have no control over.* In those days, four dollars extra meant a meal. I was always short on income. I sometimes wonder how I traveled, but being codo or tight was one way. And I did not drink. I hated alcohol.

Another fear factor kicked in—the fear of being ripped off like a gringo. The idea that south of the linea, they are always trying to rip us off because we come from the U.S. side. Mexican national vendors believe that U.S. Mexicans have just as much money as gabachos. They believe we sweep dollars up versus swinging the broom, then getting paid. In their eyes, if you are vacationing, you must be okay, because many hardworking Mexican nationals do not travel for vacation sake. After my thoughts and insecurities were overcome, I realized I had received a great deal. Custom made huaraches that actually fit me for only $18.

At first, my dark red huaraches were tight and actually made the sides of my feet bleed. I was ready to throw them away because I could not make the pain stop when I accidentally got them wet. I thought I had damaged them only to learn that after they dried, the leather had loosen up and had taken shape, according to my size 14 foot. In Mexico size, this was like a size 47. My mother and sister thought I was insane for wearing huaraches in the South Bay. Eso son de chuntaros, gente del sur. In their eyes, only provincial Mexican hicks from the center of Mexico wore these sandals. They dressed in them because that was their last choice, their only option. I wore them because I was loco. And maybe I was, but I was comfortable in them, and nobody had them.

The truth was that I wore them because they made me feel more Mexican, at a moment in my life when I felt I did not belong. How we lived in Lennox demonstrated we were inferior. Whites would not live in these conditions, why did we have to. I was an American citizen if that meant something. At least in those huaraches, I was somebody even if that somebody was still nobody.

Besides my unique fashion sense, I wore huaraches because my feet felt healthy. The more I wore them, the less toenail fungus seemed to pervade.

And happy I was for another three years until I wore them out.

I assumed that on another trip to San Felipe, I would find my huarache vendor; however, I discovered upon a return trip that he no longer existed and therefore neither did my size. My frustration made me wonder what my foot life would have been like if I had grown up in central Mexico. Barefoot? Would my feet be calloused?

I shopped and shopped for huaraches. On one occasion, when I was looking for a pair of Black cowboy boots at El Mercadito in East Los Angeles, I was told by various vendors to go to the gringo stores where they sell botas, *alli van a tener su talla*. The irony of having to go shopping where gavachos go was comical. Even worse, that was the advice from the very Mexican vendors who saw my dilemma. I had no choice but to settle for gringo footwear because only they seemed to have my size.

At last, I found a pair of those fashion sandals I would often see whites wear. When I bought them, I did so for two reasons, my size and the price of $40. I have learned that size matters more than actual cost. At least, they had my size, and I had something to wear.

When I inspected the sandals at home, I realized the following: rubber soles (which I did not like) and blue leather straps. Two straps went across the foot with buckles for tightening, and the toes were not covered. The back part of the sandal had a strap that went around the ankle. When I began to wear them, I realized that they wore just as hard as any of my previous huaraches. The rubber soles cushioned against a cork sole that pretty much resembled different leather layers that huaraches also had as foot support. And getting them to be comfortable was just as painful as the huaraches.

Some months after breaking them in but still searching for another pair of huaraches, I realized that my blue Birkenstock sandals were indeed just fancy huaraches. Nobody called them huaraches, but they were modeled exactly after them. Why would they not? These were the shoes of the ancient Mexicans, they have been wearing huaraches for thousands of years. Huaraches provided health and comfort. I might have been loco, but my loco-ness sure felt great.

One day, I will go to the Huaraches Mercado in Guadalajara and have somebody custom make me three pairs of fancy Birkenstocks for my size 15 feet.

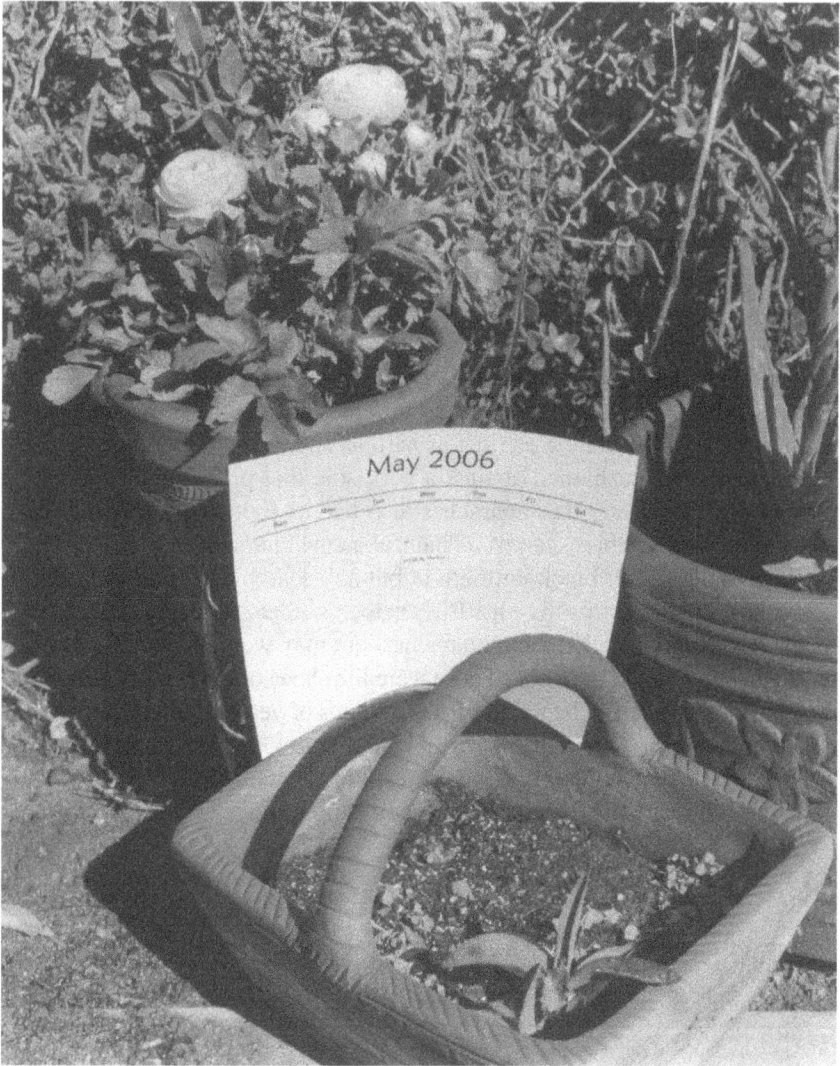

Figure 12.1.   "Mother's Day, Mother Earth"

Chapter Twelve

Mother's Day, May the 10th

For all the negativity we hear about Mexico, on one day they outshine any American holiday. May the 10th is *el dia de las madres*, Mother's Day. It is not some cop out Sunday brunch. It is a paid legal holiday. On that day, life shuts down, business as usual ceases, and mothers are celebrated for giving life, for feeding us, for scolding us. In Mexico, the mother stops the economy. The jefas have their day.

Americans do not care to recognize their mothers the same way. Americans celebrate their mothers on a day that is normally considered a day of rest or a day of worship for the superstitious lot. A two for one insincere day! That second Sunday of every May comes whether one sets the day aside for mother or not. That is disrespectful, inconsiderate, self centered, materialistic, warlike, not loving your mother perversion.

This is a dirty society, a civilization that believes mothers are worth a $5.99 breakfast at a run down Denny's or Norm's where worn out waitresses serve meals and torn vinyl booths pinch our asses; even worse, this greasy food can potentially place us on the diarrhea throne. Are mothers not worth a legal holiday that this society may set aside to spend the day together? Not here where the holidays of this country are based on wars.

Men who killed in disguise of freedom or a flag are celebrated beginning with Presidents' Day in February. When was the last time a President provided shelter or stayed up all night with a crying infant? This civilization celebrates the commander in chief even though most of them have been killers or corrupt politicians.

The next true holiday is Memorial Day for those who died in war. The soldiers who would best benefit are dead, as if they could hear or accept the fake applause. This is like being granted US Citizenship posthumously. You are dead, what good is being able to cross the border if one does not exist in

45

body? To me, Memorial Day seems more like suburban white trash fishing trips or Tijuana weekend getaways for cheap thrills.

July the 4th is a continuation of this theme; it is a celebration of war. Why people in Southern California celebrate Independence Day is beyond my comprehension because California in 1776 was not even part of the U.S., it was still colonial Mexico. When the Americans invaded, the 4th of July must be viewed more akin to the invasion day for Mexicans in California. What is there to celebrate?

And Labor Day? What a despicable holiday. A day to celebrate being worked to death. Is this day to be a break from the brutal reality that when a person ages, most of his day time will be spent laboring for somebody else? If you like the break, then maybe you are not really toiling that arduous.

And yet our mothers do not receive their societal recognition, the woman who is partially responsible for rearing decent human beings or attempting to does not have a whole Monday to herself with pay.

Veteran's Day is another war holiday set aside for those fortunate to have survived the traumas of a war. When was the last time anybody threatened the U.S. on its shores? On the other hand, the U.S. has been the aggressor to most countries with Mexicans and other Native people being victims of the empire.

Thanksgiving Day is not about war, but it is about taking—the taking of land. Still, this holiday, I like because the guajolote, sweet potatoes, and cranberries—all Mexican foods. I worship the home cooked meal. Food to me is love and life. I could care less about material possessions as long as there is comida. Since when is not eating considered healthy, much less home cooked meals prepared by our mothers?

Navidad! This is not a war day, but this figure who did not live is more recognized than a mother. Our mothers have walked on this earth, brought forth life, and deserve a legal holiday. Yet this suciedad, suicidal society celebrates paganism and virginity (if you believe that) versus fertility and the actual living. The actual god we do have.

Recently, October of 2005, the US Post Office closed in recognition of the day I despise the most—Columbus Day (Colon, a Spanish nigger). The US Post Office, state and local government, and most banks celebrate the destruction of land and the murder of thousands of native people.

Instead of celebrating more evil than the fiend was ever capable of, we should honor our mothers in October. If the US Postal Service and other government agencies are so desperate for another day off, then the least they could do is honor our mothers, not a murderer.

All I ask is to provide our mothers and jefes, fathers (they have a role too) with a societal love. All I ask is for a mother's and father's paid holiday where life ceases as we know it, and we recognize our mothers and fathers versus another day of no substance.

Chapter Thirteen

Pericos

I was driving into Rosarito one Saturday around noon when I saw an older man with his sombrero standing on a corner with five or six bright green pericos. Some of these pericos were small, some were mid-size, about the size of a hand, and two others were a lot bigger, the size of a two liter, plastic Coca-Cola bottle. The man with his brown outfit stood there with his arms stretched out almost like Christ on the cross, holding the different pericos on sticks and in cages. He had a look of anguish on his face, desperate to sell some pericos.

The pericos were magnificent with their bright green colors ready for someone to buy them. This man selling the pericos who positioned himself along the road that entered from Tijuana, hoping to convince turistas from the other side to buy pericos profoundly impacted me. Whenever I see pericos, they mesmerize me. This sense of connection is not new. From the time of my youth, I have always admired pericos, perekeetas even cuervos.

When I was eight years old, I remember my tia Lupe traveling to Mexicali and commenting how they had to smuggle their perico in. They could not get the perico to stay still in the brown bag with holes. The perico was cabron. He bit and bit and bit as he fought from being hidden and placed inside one of my tia's bags. If caught by the Border Agents, the perico would be confiscated and taken away. It was a risk they took.

Even pericos are considered undocumented, just as humans are. Fortunately, the perico was not seen, and he arrived in Inglewood to his new home and cage. He was considered special, for he could be trained to talk.

Y hablar si pudo Pocaluz style.

And soon, the perico began to talk like mi tio, Jesús:

"Chinga tu madre."

Figure 13.1. "Perico"

"Chinga tu madre."
"Pinche perico loco."
"Pinche perico loco."

Jesús (whom we called Pocaluz) laughed at his mischievousness. The perico was special, a novelty. Seeing him was like going to view some religious object, a religious object that was alive and talking. The perico was not an image concocted or the flame of some candle confused as a holy spirit.

In Mexicali, my grandparents always had perekeetas. In the early 1980s, they traveled to Leon, Guanajuato and returned with a new set of perekeetas. They were placed in the cocina where everyone noticed them. The perekeetas were even treated better than us but no worse. The house they lived in did not have air conditioning only a fan, but my grandmother made sure they were maintained fresh. My grandmother would soak a thin, white cloth made from old bed sheets and would place it over the cage to keep them cool. Fresh water and food went without saying, and even at night, they were covered for their beauty sleep as if they were children. I enjoyed seeing the interaction of those perekeetas with my 'ama although I never held them. I always associated these perekeetas with el sur de Mexico.

Later, my cousin, Antonio, had a perico, one he had bought on a trip to Sinaloa. The green perico had his wings clipped and jumped from palo to palo that was set for him in the kitchen. His strong gawks intimidated me, but I admired how my primo would allow the perico on his shoulder as if he was wearing him. The perico and Antonio were almost like one. Antonio would talk to him, and the perico acted as if he understood what he said. At best, I could tell he enjoyed sitting on Antonio's shoulder. It reminded me of the way older Native Americans wore feathers on their heads. In those years, I looked for the perico, for I knew he belonged there. He was the cross that protected mi tia Beva's kitchen and my cousin Antonio.

Still, I was afraid of pericos because I was still traumatized by the mother hen that pecked the hell out of me as a five-year-old. One day though, I overcame my fear. When I traveled into the Cuna Islands of Panama, I stayed on an island overnight where there was a beautiful perico. The way I like them, bright, bright, bright, bright green. He was on the table, and a man told me to hold him, not to fear him. The Cuna man, named Mr. Harrison, must have sensed my fear and decided to rid me of it. He told me to hold him gently and without fear on my palm.

I was hesitant, but little by little, I got closer and caressed him. As I did so, I looked out to the endless Caribbean Sea of Panama under a palapa. I really sensed a connection. The next thing I knew, I was holding him, it felt as if I was holding a baby. Even in his face and eyes, I could see his welcomeness. I could not take my eyes off of him as I cuddled him. It was a very,

very, religious moment. Ten years later, I still remember those few moments that are eternal now. This event helped me overcome my fear and confirmed a connection I have always sensed with pericos.

For Mexicans, pericos provide a religious connection to the spirit world, a spirit world not in a Christian sense but more in a human intellect. A way of existing.

Years later when I was at the oldest Pueblo in the United States, Acoma, Nuevo Mexico, I was moved by the painting inside the church of a bright yellow perico. I asked the tour guide whose name was Orlando why the painting of the perico.

Orlando explained, "This yellow parrot demonstrates our connection to our cousins in Mexico."

I was in a state of shock. Pericos enable us to see the past in the present as one. The painting confirmed that spirituality. Pericos are more than just exotic birds for Mexicans, they are our religious connection to the past, to a life that had existed for thousands of years. For Whites, these kinds of birds are more like a trophy, a bizarre bird found only in the Western Hemisphere.

Not so long ago, I was having menudo with my friend and mentor Angel Medina, and he shared with me that the double yellow head parrot almost became extinct because many of the White miners ate them during the early years of mining at the turn of the century.

And yet they, the Americans, impose artificial laws that prohibit entrance to our religious beings. In music, birds are used as wisdom and guidance in times of confusion and pain: Paloma blanca, Paloma negra, cucurrucucu, cucurrucucu, cucurrucucu, cucurrucucu, we start singing in bird language. We want to imitate the pericos, and we wish we could fly like them.

I sense in dreams we can fly like them.

Cotorrear, cotorreo, cotorro.

Even in our talk, we refer to speaking like cotorros, another kind of a perico, a little smaller with bright green and yellow feathers. Cotorreo refers to us Mexicans conversing like the cotorros. We huddle, we spread our wings get comfortable and al comadreo. We laugh, we argue, we have serious discussions, we reminisce. We congregate and are called palominas—to group like palomas.

In our cotorreo, we set council anywhere: the sidewalk, the corner, the front yard, the backyard, around the cars, any space where we need to converse. We even huddle around similar to cotorros. We are cotorros. We feel related to them. And yet, many "No loitering" signs with letters and numbers abound like crosses throughout the landscape.

Pericos are also used for cleansing rituals. They are believed to hold uncontaminated energies that many times afflict us humans. There are negative energies only they can purify and then later protect. This is why I believe all my family members and many, many, many other Mexicans have pericos, to protect us from negative vibes.

Birds are profound in the Mexican psychic. The eagle devouring the serpent is eternal, a symbol I saw on a necklace given to me at the Cherokee capital in Oklahoma that resembled old images of the aguila Mexicano. The aguila devorando la serpiente is water. The most essential substance needed for survival. The Americans have imitated the Mexicans by adopting the eagle to their passport, adopting closely related colors red, white, and blue (similar to green) for their flag and claim it as their own. We, however, live this existence, it is not for show.

Thus, the pericos are more profound than we can recognize. When I was a child my grandmother would refer to us as cuervitos, crows. My father bragged how handsome his sons were, and my Mayo grandmother who once called me Papago because of my look stated to my father: "Eso fue lo que decia el cuervo de los suyos." Our humor and comparisons are often made to crows, the bird life as they all laughed.

As I drove past the old man selling pericos, my cousin Jesus (Pocaluz' son) announced: "I'm going to come and buy un chingo para vender al otro lado."

Weeks later, he bought ten and snuck them across the border. He sold them in a month, but as pericos are hard work, he tired of his adventure. And yet according to him, they all sold to people in Bell Gardens in the surrounding areas all by word of mouth, quietly and secretively so we can worship without fear of castigo.

Jews can circumcise their boys, Americans can torture cows by making veal, voodoo rituals of chicken slaughters are permitted, and yet we Mexicans cannot bring our religious beings over legally for fear of confiscation and denial of our heritage. Freedom of association, yeah right!

Whites have almost extinguished our spiritual beings, our connection to the past. Erase the past—that is what they have done since they got here. And erase they continue.

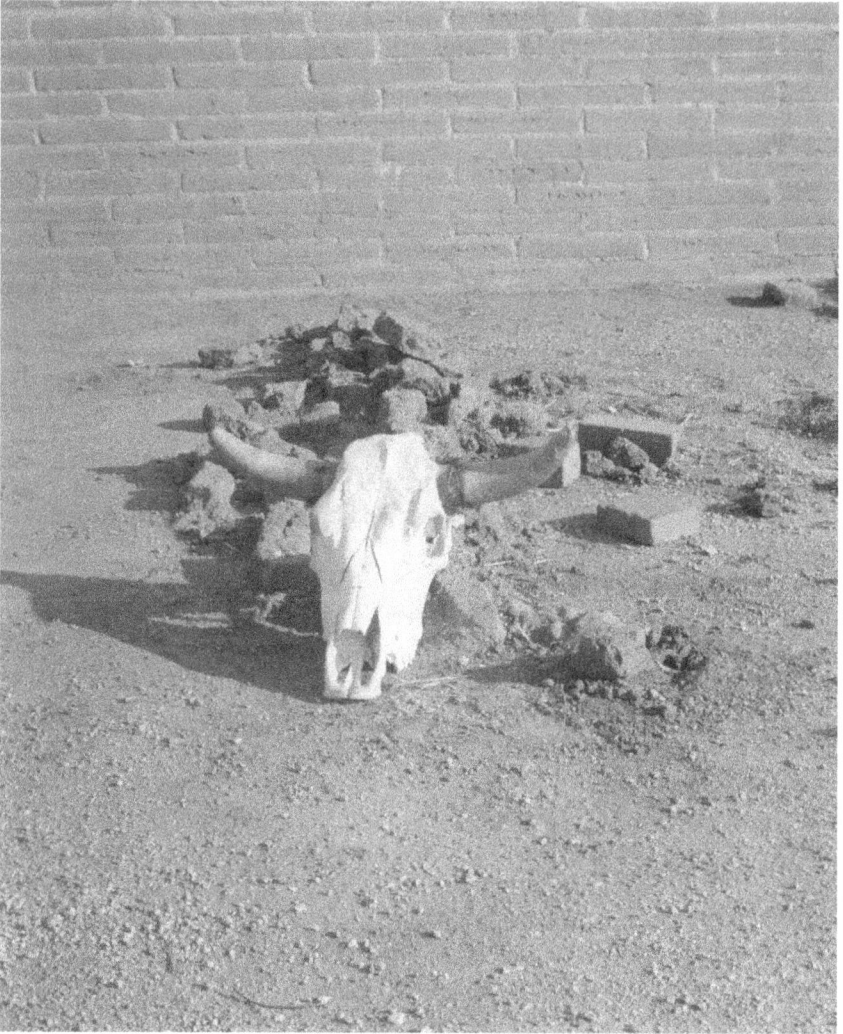

Figure 14.1. "Bull Skull"

Chapter Fourteen

Bullfights

One day bullfights must be reinstated in California. As was once reported in the *Los Angeles Times*, there existed a bullring in front of what is now the Los Angeles City Hall. One day I want to be able to yell, "Ole," as the bull rushes the bullfighter in Alta California.

Bullfighting is the eternal battle of man and woman. The man is the bull, the matador is the woman. The matador (or woman) thinks that she can outsmart the bull. Sometimes, she can; other times, she cannot.

There is honor in poniendo cuernos.

Life is like a bullfight, I face el toro with fear. I know he is charging at me, and I must confront and stab him before he horns me to death.

In this society, the bullfight can be explained another way: the eternal battle between cultures. In this case, Mexicans are the bull, the US is the matador. The matador (or US) thinks that he can outsmart the bull, smother it, oppress it, tease it, then kill it. Sometimes, he can, but the bull always fights back, his anger serves him well, his wounds fuel his fire. The bull fights to live; if he dies, his bones remain and remind.

This bull will not die at the hand of a suicidal society.

Figure 15.1. "Cuco"

Chapter Fifteen

Peleas de Gallos (Cockfighting)

In a backyard somewhere in Lennox, Mexican men, some young, others old, form a large circle quietly cheering the fighting roosters. Two roosters face each other with a small blade on one claw of each fowl, each will fight cruelly for survival.

Ponle atencion a la jura. Somebody keeps an eye out for the sheriffs.

One cockfight is over. Some men win, and others have lost. Maybe next time.

The next round will start soon, a new set of roosters. The trainers are ready to test their training skills. They whisper to the rooster, speaking to him behind the dark brown feathers and listen he does. For as soon as the orders are given, each one heeds his commands and instantly begins to fight. How much training, how much running, how much conditioning has gone into play? How much feet jabbing for the blade to slice some feathers and skin, to slit that throat and be declared the winner?

The crowd cheers and cheers. Who could ever imagine humans cheering and applauding almost worshipping fowls? It could be worse, they could be superstitious and paganistic by praying to a piece of wood, representing a make-believe figure who has never existed and whose mother was still a virgin after giving birth. Ni madre, aqui adoran al gallo. The rooster could make them some money, their prayers could soon be answered.

The gallos flutter back and forth, thrusting themselves into each other with wings expanded hopefully strengthened from training, wishing for that one hit all need to strike it rich. The cheering gets louder, the dust rises in the air from the pushing off from the floor when all of sudden someone screams: "La chota, la chota, la chota."

Like cucarachas, the men flee, the old men become acrobatic and jump over a five foot wall somehow. They had not raised their legs that high in 25 years,

12 year olds follow their fathers or uncles and become fugitives by way of observation. Would an excuse of "mi papa me llevo" work in front of a judge?

The festive Palenque is over. It was already underground; this jovial ritual of cockfighting, betting, camaraderie, mutual cultural interest will lay dormant for a few days or until another secluded backyard can be found. Hopeful bets must wait, and others continue training their rooster for the next tournament.

The old man Gus who hopped the wall returns to his laundry where he arrives at 4 AM to exercise the rooster in the alley. The rooster is continuously walked back and forth, back and forth, back and forth, back and forth. He is fed well according to rooster standards; after eating, he continues to expand his lungs. Back and forth and back and forth.

"Este gallo vale $300 dolares."

The gallo exercises more, for Gus is addicted to gambling. He gambles to win but plays for the adrenaline.

The rooster is well taken care of, he is celebrated and respected, yet the chota prosecutes men for illegally fighting roosters. They must pay a misdemeanor. American laws and American courts are nothing but a new form of the Inquisition, the Holy Office of the Inquisition.

Five generations back, Mexicans openly fought roosters along with ranchera music, food, and cerveza in California. Now Americans are concerned about humane treatment.

Americans concerned about humane treatment? They consume more chickens than chickens can be produced. They inject them with steroids and then slit their throats for their salmonella diet on the conveyor belt. At least, in cockfighting, the rooster can prolong his life depending on his fighting skills; if he loses, he is buried entirely. Other times, the gallo becomes a pet in the backyard until a cat or coyote gets to him or worse an oncoming vehicle. A Mexican rooster can live a long time. An American chicken does not even get a name.

Humane treatment? The death penalty is carried out in this country at alarming rates. Many innocent people—including mentally handicap people—have been executed. As many as 107 people have been exonerated for false convictions sometimes days away from the lethal injection. The Fourth Reich continues to use the death penalty.

Humane treatment? Boxing is a sport here. Two human beings, generally poor, Mexican or Black occasionally a Filipino or a Russian but never a suburban white male, can literally beat their brains into destruction and that is acceptable. It is prime time in Las Vegas; beautiful bikinis announcing the new rounds, million dollar venues, boxing thugs attempting to look respectable by wearing suits and endless gambling, but no cockfighting is allowed?

Humane treatment? We allow the toughest of the boys to play football and run the risk of breaking their legs and necks, and that is acceptable. We applaud when the hit is vicious as the body jerks outward and the head inward. I saw a football player die in front of me during a high school football game.

Humane treatment? Why are White men allowed to hunt and kill deer, moose or duck for a sport? All because it is acceptable and based on what right, their right to carry a rifle under the 2nd Amendment which they wrote.

Humane treatment? What about circumcision? Has anybody asked those newborn boys if they want that thumb-size guillotine chopping off their foreskin which serves as a natural gland protector and permits full penis erection? Has anybody asked that screaming little boy if the guillotine that clipped the tip of his penis was necessary for religion? Can he choose his religion at one day old when he is only concentrating on that nipple which is his life line? Has the baby's penis been so sexualized at one day old that under the disguise of religion and science must inflict such brutal pain? That infant was better off inside the womb, this world is too damn cruel.

And they prosecute Mexican men for fraternizing around cultural rituals Americans find deplorable. Yet, nobody villianizes their traditions. Before Americans came to California, cockfighting was normal; now it is persecuted and forced underground as are many other traditions in this land of the free.

Misdemeanors are worth paying for cultural survival. The search for greater secrecy continues in somebody's backyard where nobody would ever suspect they are cockfighting.

Figure 16.1. "Reuben"

Chapter Sixteen

Reuben de Jesús

Reuben de Jesús is my friend, one of my compas who I met once in a class I taught via his imposing comments. I did not always agree with what he said, but I liked that he had courage from the back of classroom to state his opinion. His comments were not incorrect; he just had his own point-of-view. From the back of the room to my left, I could view his eyes looking up. His eyes bugged out, glowing from his chocolate hue skin. Our friendship began that spring semester of 1998.

At first, we did not really share much, we just hung out at East Los Angeles College, but the more we talked, the more I began to learn from him and about him. I learned: Reuben was a Marine for six years, he was a reserve when we met; his mother had attended Garfield High School in East Los Angeles as he had; and he was a math wiz.

Reuben has taught me that family is a verb, mutually. He has demonstrated that family can be those people who share the same values, morality, carnalismo—a brotherhood not based on the same birth canal that brought us out, rather a kinship much like to a marriage. In Los Angeles, other Mexicans can come to be more your family more than your blood relatives including some of our very own brothers.

While attending Garfield High School, Reuben was enrolled in the accelerated Escalante Program. As a student in this program, he saw many flaws in the esteemed program that were not revealed in *Stand and Deliver*—the Hollywood version of students in East LA excelling in math and taking the AP exam. The first point of conflicting information is that there was more than one teacher in the program. The Bolivian, Jaime Escalante, was not even the better teacher, although he took credit for the increases in math scores. The better teachers were two other guys named Mr. Villavicencio and Mr. Benjamin Jimenez, neither of whom were given credit.

Another flaw was the dirty little secret that Escalante would select the best math students from the local junior high schools, which means he selected well-prepared students to "demonstrate" major pedagogical advances. Not factored in these successes were the end results of educational struggles from the late 1960s that aimed to improve the educational arena for Mexican students.

Another point of interest about the Escalante Program is that Escalante was a right-wing Republican who was anti-bilingual education and was a favorite of then Governor Pete Wilson who pushed for Proposition 187. Plus according to Benjamin Jimenez (a former Escalante Program teacher who now teaches in the Math Department at Santa Monica College), Escalante was a bigot towards Mexicans. And last, in the mid-1990s, Escalante was pushed out of the program.

For Reuben, being in the Escalante Program was not easy. While he did well in math, the program disregarded other courses, one being English which Reuben was failing. When I asked him how he could have been failing English, his answer was simple: "The calculus courses required so much homework that I did not have enough time to read and complete my English assignments."

Reuben barely graduated from high school due to his grades in English, even though he had received A's in calculus. Even with successful grades in math, he could still not be accepted into a state college because of his low grades in English. Thus, Reuben's example begs the question: What good is an honor's program in a high school if it fails to teach students how to balance all schoolwork? Reuben's example proves the need to critique all educational programs, even the highly esteemed ones.

As more time continued, I learned that Reuben did not come from an impoverished family. He grew up in East Los Angeles, but his mother had been a home owner, had completed three years of college at Cal State Los Angeles, and had even once traveled to Hawaii after when his grandfather passed away. Reuben's mother's economic situation was based on two factors: one, she was an only child, and two, his abuelito had been a drug dealer, a fact that Reuben was not embarrassed to admit. When his grandfather died, his mother inherited some of the property.

For Reuben, his father was his abuelito. He was a tough belt loving abuelo who owned a small store by the Ramona Garden Courts and let him and his brothers splurge from Doritos and Twinkies. Reuben can remember seeing his abuelo shoot at some cholos who were trying to hold him up. When his grandfather died, Reuben's father figure died, Reuben became orphaned at age 12. Reuben knew little of his father other than that he was Native American.

When Reuben told me that he lost his only father so young, I could relate to him, for I too lost my father at a young age. Reuben is the eldest of four, and all of them fought for limited attention from his mother, as did I. Maybe we understood each other that way. Talking about our fathers was fascinating and yet painful. Nature took mine away and anger his, my father died of an aneurysm and his split after his mother wanted nothing to do with him. Reuben would mention that his father did not fight for him and maybe so, but the children belong to the mothers not the fathers; men are inconsequential, sperm donors.

We continued to laugh, talk, check out the rucas, plus another guy named Manny was part of the gang. We learned and socialized simultaneously. We talked about women from our past. One day, as we drank coffee and hung out, I asked Reuben why he joined the Marines and did not go to college directly.

Reuben's response caught me off guard. He explained: "Look bro, when I graduated from high school, my mother kicked me out of the house and into the garage which had been converted into a studio. She kicked me out of the house, charged me $300 rent not even one month after graduating. She told me this would make me responsible. So I joined the Marines as a reserve because I needed to pay the rent. You know how people say that Mexicans are family-oriented. Bullshit. I was told to be responsible with no tools and yet my mother inherited her house and money. She was given a head start, I wasn't."

Through Reuben, I learned that not all Mexican families are the same. His mother, Eva, had inherited two sets of apartments and a certain amount of cash, but Reuben was almost made homeless under her desire to make him "work hard," "be responsible," and "earn it the old fashion way"—the way she did not. What was worse was this one-room studio had a bathroom with a toilet and shower, but it did not have a kitchen, so the loncheras were his home meals. A home meal is lujo for him, a luxury.

Another commonality between Reuben and me is our self-serving siblings. My mother did not kick me out at eighteen, but she sure sides with her mijos who are more of a burden on her, as does Reuben's mother. Our mothers take sides with the problematic siblings, the ones who deceive or cheat. They defend their mijos blindly.

As I got to know Reuben, he was continuing his education. Reuben attended East Los Angeles College and then later trade schools where he became certificated in Electricity and Plumbing. During 1999–2000, Reuben demonstrated to me what a true friend is. I was rejected for tenure at East Los Angeles College. The battle started as a clash over personalities, but when I fought back against the old timers in the Chicano Studies Department, they banded together with the administration and ran a smear campaign against me even spreading rumors about sexual improprieties (all of which were untrue).

Reuben having been in four of my classes and always present could attest to their lies. But just as important, he provided me with guidance when nobody

else was willing to listen. He did it by sharing his own experiences. He told me
of an incident: when he was in the Marines, he was abandoned by his com-
manding officer in the deserts of Twenty-Nine Palms. He told me that after exercises, the unit was resting for the night. When he woke up the next morning,
he discovered that they had left him behind with no food or water. The man
was left for dead by the organization that professes to be faithful, the joke of
Semper-Fi. If not for a patrol unit who spotted him, he would have died in the
high desert. The patrol who found him complained to his commander, and
when Reuben returned to the Encino Base, the commander blackballed
Reuben. Then, he transferred to the Pico Rivera base. Reuben only ran into
more trouble because of word of mouth from one commander to another.

Reuben summed up his experiences: "I should have remained in Encino to
fight the lies upfront versus agreeing to move to another unit and have the
other commander think of me as a problem. He only heard one side, so when
I arrived there, I was already tainted. I suggest you stay at ELAC and fight
this head on because if they transfer you, they will smear your name and you
will be guilty wherever you go."

Reuben's words were biblical. When I did transfer, I was viewed as a per-
vert and a problem. When we went to arbitration, Reuben testified on my behalf and rebutted the district's attorney head on by telling them that he heard
the president of the college state to me that the rumors smeared me and no
matter what I did whether legal or not I was not going to return to ELAC.
Reuben not only testified to hearing those words, but he refuted the German
Jew Nigger attorney's claim to favoritism by pointing to his transcripts as
proof that he had received a couple of C's in my classroom. There was no favoritism there, just fighting for what was right. Seven students, two females
and two faculty members testified and fought on my behalf because they
learned and found somebody similar to them. I had no resources to continue
fighting because the faculty union did not represent me (a union to which I
paid dues and that claimed in its literature to "support" faculty) and sided
with the district. The Italian Nigger arbitrator ruled against me, but what did
I expect the district and union paid his fees.

Reuben was my biggest support in my dark hours, saving me from this suicidal society, from the joke of the legal system, from suicide itself.

I learned a bitter lesson in life that Mexicans—like Whites—will stick a
knife in your back and will cut deals with those Whites in charge. My hope
nonetheless was based on the fact that ten people testified on my behalf including a White person and a Black person who believed I was being unjustly
terminated.

And Reuben was there. He was there for me as my brother. With this support, I moved on, away from that society that wanted to kill me, that wanted
me suicidal.

Even as I went through that difficult time, Reuben began to go through a hard time himself. Around this time, I was shocked to learn that he told me he had two children whom he never saw. Apparently, Reuben had been asking his ex to see his children for months, and months dragged into years. In 1998, he filed for visitation rights, but nothing ever came of it. Then, he went to court again in 2000 only to be slapped with a $20,000 bill for child support. On top of that, the DA had his license suspended.

Child custody laws make no sense. The district attorney suspended his driver's license thereby limiting his ability to work and even see his children but wanted him to pay a bill of $20,000. Reuben had to quit his job because he feared getting pulled over without a license. In order to reinstate his license, Reuben went on General Relief. General Relief reinstated his license and put a halt to his ever-mounting debt.

Although Reuben had not seen his daughter, Sara, and his son, Daniel, when they were infants nor was he allowed to be a part of their lives, he owed child support. Monica (his ex) would not allow him to visit nor did she bring the children over to him—even though he asked her over and over for years. Reuben could not afford an attorney, but he wanted to be a part of his children's lives.

Of course, after hearing this story from my friend, I had to ask, "How did you end up with two kids from this woman?"

Reuben's side of the story was: "We were not ever attempting to get pregnant, or so I was told. She would visit with me, and when we would have sex, she would say that she was on the pill. At first, I hesitated, but when she reassured me, why would I reject great sex especially in the morning? I did not go to her home, she came to my studio. Once my daughter was born, I wanted to see her and the only way was to make Monica happy. She made promises, that I would see Sara soon, but she lied again and then my son was born. The best part is now the puta professes to be a Born-Again Christian, but what I wonder is: Where was her morality when she was lying about being on the pill? Look man, I don't regret it because I have my kids, but the district attorney makes it harder for me to be a father. The district attorney only wants me to be an ATM and cares nothing about my side of the story or my rights as a father."

What does this say about this suicidal society? Why are some Mexican women now thinking in White terms: What's in it for me? How can I take advantage of the system even when I am deceitful? After all, do the children not belong to the father? In California, the answer is no, the law makes sure that they do not.

And this is what I admire about Reuben; he fights for what is right while he questions his place in this society, the irrationality, the exploitation, the inequity.

Reuben is a learned person. He informs himself, he reads. Reuben knows more about World War II history than any of the professors I had at both UCLA and USC, and I majored in Political Science and Urban Planning. He is concerned about Mexicans in California, he is also proud to be Mexican. He makes me laugh when he explains, "Bro, I have never been to Mexico, Rosarito is California and I like my buche, tacos de cabeza, sesos, mis tortas, that is why I love East Los Angeles, I don't need to go to Mexico, I already live here. Y tu sabes that I like Jose Alfredo Jimenez, he died the year I was born."

Reuben speaks Spanish. He is not one of those third generation Mexicanos who speak English only. His mother was born in Jalisco, but his grandmother, the mother of his mother, was born in Los Angeles. Migrations do not only go north, they also travel south.

After three generations, he is the poorest yet the most proud and spiritually centered of all his family. He can deconstruct the evils of Christianity better than anybody I have ever met. One time, Reuben argued with a Black woman who was studying law at UCLA and was a Baptist who believed in Jesus. Reuben told her confidently, "Why would I believe in myths and legends from another continent? Do you not think we had our own belief system here. As a Native American, I did not have to depend on customs from the "chosen" people. What made them special? We had our own spirituality here and I know because I am native."

I was amazed at how strong his argument was. He negated the Baptist's point of view with a cultural rationality; plus by societal standards, she was more educated than him. He proved that educational institutions are more about faux status and entertain superstitious facts. His thinking parallels mine, we are Mexican Apaches of the north who must continue to fight for cultural survival and against ignorance even among our own.

In July of 2002, Reuben showed his true character. I awoke early one morning to the coughing of my six-month-old Chihuahua (son of Simon and Cihua whom I named Cahua/warrior). Cahua kept coughing and coughing, and eventually he died in my arms. I lost a life that belonged to me in my arms. That day was extremely painful. I buried him inside a box on the side of the house wrapped in a white towel.

That day seemed eternal. My other canines, Simon, the father, would not go near me and Tixoc, the uncle, would lay on top of the tomb of Cahua. It was the darkest day I have lived through, and I saw my father die.

For some reason, Cahua's death was painful. I felt part of me die; maybe that death was meant for me, and he protected me. I am a straight Indio, I do believe I am related to the animal world, as equals. I know that my Chihuahuas protect my spirit. When I called Reuben, he showed up in the afternoon. I could not cry anymore, but tranquility I did find.

Reuben just hung out with me, helped me build a brick flower bed and made me feel secure, like an older brother. Time healed the lost of Cahua. Reuben is the brother I wish I had. My cuate who guides me and protects me, my counselor and even my teacher, the best professor I have had. I admire him because he acts from the heart. If not for him, I would not have been able to fix much in my home or enjoy a good cup of coffee with ease.

Over the years I have known Reuben, he has worked as a casino security guard, a strip club bouncer, a radio promoter, and a forklift driver for Goodyear before they closed shop in Commerce in 2000 and moved to Victorville. Reuben—like all Mexicans—does what it takes to survive, he is always thinking about what he can do, plumbing, carpentry, selling real estate.

Reuben's struggles disturb me because here is this person who is bilingual, certificated in electricity and plumbing but more unemployed than employed. He loves his children, will bend backwards if treated kindly and yet still lives in the same garage studio with no kitchen.

Reuben once said before the George W. Bush re-election, "2004 has been a year of no progress, I have gone backward in this so called land of opportunity."

The day prior to Christmas Eve Reuben was called to go work for a plumbing company, and fortunately his mother loaned him the $300 union fee. He did work after Christmas. Now we'll wait and see. He sees his kids too, two weekends a month.

When I see Mexicans like Reuben, I cannot help but think of Samuel Huntington's depressing but poignant data on third and fourth generation Mexicans—according to Huntington, third and fourth generation Mexicans are more apt at failure because America has no human space for them even in the work space. Reuben is a true reflection of those Mexicans who are stuck in the racial caste structure of California. It is the third and fourth generation Mexicans in the US who are digressing economically but are more nationalistic Mexican than anybody south of the border.

Reuben's case demonstrates that this society is more vicious to second, third, fourth generation Mexicans than even the undocumented. Reuben's case reveals the twisted legal system and how we can turn on each other or use each other. Reuben's story accounts for the suicide in this society. And yet, Reuben's story provides a glimmer of hope, he hopes and dreams as we all do.

"Chido, chido!"

Figure 17.1.   "The Border at Night"

Chapter Seventeen

A Day Crossing the Border

Late in the evening sometime in the middle of the week, I was driving to Mexicali to visit my sister. My sister was waiting for my arrival, but as is accepted, I was late. If I say one hour, it could mean two hours or even four hours. Part of the problem is that I have a urinating dilemma; I have to constantly go since I drink too much coffee. I pull off of the highway numerous times, once in Cabazon, once in Indio, once in Brawley. Sometimes, I eat, other times I just get more coffee. Every so often, I stop and visit my paternal abuela in El Centro and then drive into Mexicali from El Centro.

My sister is my last connection to Mexico. In this part of Mexico, there is more of a connection with the US than to the rest of Mexico. After all, the fact remains that Mexicali sits along the California peninsula detached from the mainland; Mexico City is 2500 miles away. This geography demands the flow of goods between the two sides: people flow, goods flow.

My sister is one of those strange characters who embodies two naturalizations. She is a resident of Mexico for having been born in the Mexican half of California, but simultaneously she has been a US resident since the early 1970s. Her whole life has revolved around this duality. Part of my sister's duality results from her upbringing by my mother's parents (My mother moved to Los Ángeles after having my sister in order to support her). Another part of her duality is having five younger brothers who have been born and raised in Los Ángeles.

My sister was able to receive residency as the daughter of my mother, and my mother received residency when I was born. With this residency, my sister can freely cross the wall that separates the poorer from the wealthier half of California. She can move freely or as freely as the US permits.

My sister's husband, however, waited over twenty years before applying for his residency. He had too much pride in seeking US residency from my sister. Call it machismo, *orgullo*, too much pride, but he waited and did it on his own. Until this day, he has yet to seek employment in the Imperial Valley even though he has the right to do so. Indeed, the issue of residency through marriage remains a great fear among Mexicans, men and women. Many fear abandonment after a marriage, perhaps a child, and then a green card. Marrying someone without residency is taboo.

When my sister gave birth to her two children, she did so in Los Ángeles County. Three months after each one was born, she returned to her husband who stayed behind to work and mind the house. Due to my sister's desire to secure her children's future employment eligibility, her children also have a dual existence. Even still, at first, my sister's actions resulted in headaches. The older child was forced to seek permission from the state government to go to school because he was a US citizen. After fighting to obtain this permission for her son, my sister secured a Mexican birth certificate for my niece to avoid future headaches. A family doctor signed the paper work.

For my sister and her family, life in Mexicali was better than our life in Lennox. One reason was that they lived in a home with three bedrooms, (the property was bought by my mother because her parents also lived there until their deaths). That house was built in the mid 1970s on an acre of land. Although the streets in the *colonia* were unpaved therefore dusty and muddy when it rained, my nephew and my niece had an acre to play on.

When my niece vacationed in Los Ángeles with her grandmother, the difference was clear. Life was spent in the barrios of Lennox, a *Tepito (a slum in Mexico City)* version of Los Angeles. She knew the dump of both sides of the border. When she visited her grandmother in Lennox, she watched television while cars blew exhaust into the house because people parked right at the door, six inches away from the entrance. There was no room to play; the cars took up all that space.

That was why my sister never moved. Employment might be limiting in the Imperial Valley, but they lived in a larger, less cramped house with space for children to play.

Still, there was one factor of reality that my sister grappled with—the education of her children. When the children were young, they attended *escuela primaria* (elementary school) y *secundaria* (junior high school) in Mexicali. My sister knew that by high school, her kids would have to either move to Los Ángeles or cross into Calexico. Their high school diplomas after all would also aid in their future employment prospects and would keep them away from the back-breaking labor in agriculture, something my sister did and still does.

My sister knew the border routine from life experience; she has worked as a day laborer on a celery farm on and off for several years. She also knew that border crossing was time-consuming, demanding, and energy-draining. As a result, when her son was fifteen and ready for high school, she sent him to live with his grandmother in Lennox. My sister sent her son for a "better life" but shattered her family in doing so. Her son was just fifteen, and he struggled tremendously—school was not his priority, she was not around to discipline, feed, and nurture him. Living in Lennox depressed him as did living with my youngest brother with whom he would clash. He was lonely, and hearing the grandmother gripe was not pleasing either. After one year, he had had enough. He ventured home to Mexicali. My sister learned that her son's well-being was more important than his high school diploma.

Later, due to my sister's resourcefulness, a lady at work agreed to help out—a deal was cut. This co-worker of my sister's lent her address in Calexico in order for my nephew to go to Calexico High School, located in the northeast corner of the city in exchange for her claiming him as a dependent.

Consequently, the duality of my nephew would play out everyday for the next three years. My sister or her husband would give him a ride to the *cruzero*, the railroad crossings where he would take the bus or a taxi to the border crossing. Then, he walked the rest of the way. In total, this was a one-hour journey of ten miles, and classes started at 8 AM.

For those who say, *Hey, this kid can't go to school here. He doesn't even live here, his parents don't pay taxes.* I say bullshit, a la chingada. A school district may be as anal about residency as possible, but lots of people cheat. First of all, there are the people who "borrow" an address in order to go to a certain school as opposed to the one to which they are assigned. School politics—you must go to this school, that school is the worst. Secondly, what about the US citizens who don't pay taxes but send their children to school. The IRS doesn't bust everyone. Third, since schools are mainly funded by property taxes, are we then to say only the children of property owners can go to school? Only a suicidal society would allow such an extreme caste system to prevail. Then again, we may not be far off from that extreme.

The real problem is of course these societal laws do not account for the complexity of the border, the flow that gives it life. Why doesn't this society account for an American citizen who lives on the other side? Is he not to be counted because his address reads Baja California versus California? Is the state not obligated to provide education regardless of address? What if he were homeless?

Furthermore, regarding taxes, consider the following: my sister has paid taxes working in the celery fields (taxes which by the way go to improve roads, etcetera that she does not use), my mother, his grandmother, has paid taxes for over forty years, his grandfather paid taxes, his uncles (five to be exact) all work and pay taxes, his great-grandfather paid taxes picking cotton in

Winterhaven, and of course, he would be a tax-payer himself in the future. In fact, I would argue that his education had already been paid for, three generations back.

My nephew did graduate from high school. Currently, he attends community college, works at McDonald's (a job that is hard to get in the area and that deducts state and federal taxes from his paycheck), and lives at home. My nephew is one of the thousands, I do mean thousands of people who cross the border to work, but who live on the Mexican side due to the high cost of living in the US. This border phenomenon is not new. I doubt it will change any time soon either.

That was all I knew of the duality that day I arrived at my sister's house. Traffic and the last ten miles of driving on the highway toward San Felipe took a toll on me. The journey to my sister's house always takes me through the *terregal de California*. Contrary to popular belief, *el sur de California* is a very dusty place, southern California rains dust.

There, I found my sister, her daughter, her son, her husband, and their Polish sheepdog who gets his hair blow-dried every week.

"Por fin. Llegaste."

There is no greater feeling than arriving to that dusty home where life seems to remain timeless. The wooden outhouse, the cerco (wooden fence) that remains upright but faded from the hot summer days, the junkyard collection my brother-in-law has accumulated to make his Chevy truck live longer, the overgrown mesquite that seems to smoother us in hugs and the half-completed brick home that my sister and husband were building for themselves only to see their money dry up.

I got a bear hug from my sister, nephew, brother-in-law and niece. Even Cori, the Polish sheepdog, jumped on me and greeted me as if his uncle.

"Cori, estate en paz," my sister scolded him.

After some tacos, I volunteered to take my niece, Lupe, (who was then a sophomore at Calexico High School following her brother's tradition) to school the next day, so she could stay up with us a little longer.

"Yo te llevo mija," I said.

"Si, pero bien temprano."

"Bueno pues, me levantas."

When the alarm—my niece knocking on the door—went off, I thought, "Chingado, what had I committed myself to?" I should know my limits; I am not a morning person. I believe that rising up early is for slave purposes. Who in his right mind does not want to sleep in until 9 AM? Who in his right mind wants to wake up at 5 or 6 AM? In fact, I have always believed God punishes the poor by making us get up before the sun comes out. The sun should wake us up not the clock or some schedule another fucking human being has established.

"Julián, nos tenemos que ir antes de la 7 porque la cruzada va estar pesada. Va mucha gente a trabajar."

The crossing would be congested because there were many cars heading into the factory fields to work. Everybody wants to get there on time. And my niece was no different; she was being "trained" to be on time.

We left the house by 7 AM, and what was hard to imagine was that my niece normally leaves at 6:30 AM.

"Mira si llego tarde me van a castigar despues de la escuela."

I learned years ago that punctuality is a convenience for somebody else. Schools train kids for their future jobs, and the jobs expect workers, former students, to be punctual. They say it's about responsibility, but whose responsibility are we talking about? When traffic holds us back, who is responsible? If there is an accident, should the person responsible pay back everyone he made late? What about when a bus is late? Is the driver to hand out notes to departing passengers?

"Chale mija, no te preocupes. Yo entro contigo. Mejor vamos al café y una Dona."

"Deberas? Tu te haces responsable?"

"Claro, mejor vamos a comer."

At that moment, I felt I didn't have to rush through all the traffic on Avenida Justo Sierra. I would not have to zig zag, for I was still partially asleep, my body ached. We could now converse.

"Mija, como te gusta la escuela?"

"Las clases estan bien."

"Tienes amigos y amigas? Van otros campañeros de Mexicali?"

My interfering questions do not give her time to answer.

"Los que pasamos diariamente somos los cuidadanos, los que son residentes se quedan en Calexico porque tienen miedo que les quiten la mica." The daily crossers like me are U.S. citizens; those that stay in Calexico are U.S. residents. They are afraid the INS will revoke their US residency cards.

"Oye, y son pinches los emigrantes?" Are the border officers assholes?

"Depende, si nos conocen no? Hasta te dan preferencia en la pasada, verdad, simon? Pero si son cabrones, te la hacen de mas. Una vez un pinche chino me pregunto porque no hablaba ingles. Le dije que vivia en Mexicali y me detuvo 15 minutos. Le dije que era cd. Americana y que el ingles no tenia nada que ver. Le dije que tenia hambre y que ibamos al cine. Se le hacia increible que no hablaba ingles. Al cabo no me gusta."

For my niece and many others, daily border passing depends on the border agents themselves. Some may let you pass preferentially. Others are assholes who act out. One Chinese American agent tried to hold my niece back once because she didn't speak English. My niece told him that speaking English was not a requirement for being a US citizen. The Chinese American could not hold her back very long, but he said, "How can you not speak English and be a U.S. citizen?"

Obviously, that agent had never been to Chinatown in San Francisco where many residents rarely speak English; furthermore, if they do speak English, it is very, very hard to understand. It isn't any version of English I understand.

Plus, what that agent and others like him fail to understand is that the Imperial Valley is an animal unto itself. It is the most Mexican county percentage wise in the state of upper California. English is not necessary for survival.

My niece cracked me up when she stated she didn't like to speak English either. When I asked her why, she said: "Nos divide." It divides us.

She further explained, "Porque las que aprenden ingles se creen superior a los que no. Me caen gordos los que pretenden hablar íngles, hasta los maestros." Those that learn English consider themselves superior than the Spanish only speaking people. I can't stand those that pretend to speak English only, including the teachers.

Her words woke me up instantly. I was being lectured on the border, a place I hate but have known all of my life. Her commentary on English amazed me. Most people believe English is so vital. As a result of this process of turning us into Brown Gringos for minimum wage, we are trained to hate each other. This hatred was clear; this fifteen-year-old kid knew what she was saying, learning English was already dividing her age group.

As I kept driving, I realized attending high school this way, living in this duality was a major challenge because of distance, transportation, bureaucracy of two countries (both state and federal), society.

Eight miles later, we ran right into the United States. It is not a very welcoming place. One literally runs into an eighteen foot high metal pole fence that looks like a prison. We were leaving the penal complex or entering, depending on your perspective.

While in line, I noticed that most of the cars had California license plates from the US side. It was 7:30 AM, and the line moved slowly but consistently.

"Oye, y no te cansas cruzar todo los dias?"

"Te acostumbras y por eso llego cansada."

"Salgo a las 3 p.m. y me vengo con la bola."

"Tomo el camion, y para las 5 p.m. llego, hago mi tarea y antes de las 7:30 p.m. a dormir para levantarme a las 5:30 a.m. Esa es mi rutina."

Soon, we could see the first houses of Calexico. The view these homes have consists of the metal fence, the crossing vehicles, and the houses from

Mexicali facing north. Mexicans on both sides face each other as if visiting one another in jail.

Finally, the border patrol posed the question of the day. We responded: "American Citizen, American Citizen." It was 8:15 AM.

"Chale con llegar a tiempo, vamos a tomar un café y pan dulce. Los molletes estaban ricos."

"Si."

I drove through the dead of Calexico, a city no one can really boast about.

In the school office, I said to the attendance office clerk, "My niece is behind schedule because I was late."

The English-speaking Mexican lady gave her a pass to class, and I walked her in with no problem, no tardiness, just a great conversation about the border that began in one country and was carried out in the classrooms of Calexico High School in another country.

At the end of that day, my niece would wait for the bus that would drop her off at the border crossing, where she would walk and catch another bus or a taxi home to her colonia.

Many of the people who live close to the border flow back and forth as a necessity, a survival of the strongest. The border divides us physically, spiritually, mentally. The border permits the suicidal society to rip, tear, sever our souls.

A la chingada con Estados Unidos de America.

Figure 18.1. "Selling Documents"

Chapter Eighteen

Acting Names

This story is based on truth; however, names have been changed in order to protect the innocent.

How does a person survive being undocumented in Los Angeles? How do you avoid the migra, get a driver's license, a green card, a social security number all the while keeping your original identity uncontaminated and unblemished?

The answer: You become Hollywoodized. You become an actor; the set is real life, your scene: survival. Not survivor, survival! You do what self-centered egotistical actors do: change your name, your identity, your hair, your sexual preference (depending), your body to skeletal thin. The name should somehow captivate for that cheap chance at a commercial to be asked for the better movie role. Being white is essential, Jewish preferable. The new name works even with much competition.

If you are an undocumented Mexican, not an Amexican (that is a US born or raised Mexican), word of mouth is to go to Huntington Park, Mac Arthur Park, any park where Mexicans congregate. All open spaces are open for sale: elotes, champurrado, cobijas, almuadas, cd de musica o peliculas, micas, licencias, mota, coca de lo todo. Affordable, cheaper than the real documents.

Here, the film starts.

In the park, you become an American citizen. It's simple.

A vendor says to a man alone, "What do you need?'

"Todo los documentos."

"Okay, it'll cost you $200 and 2 hours of time," the vendor says.

You give him pictures and half of the money, $100 dollars. Two hours later, he returns with the documents, you pay the rest of the fee. Now you're an American citizen.

Your stage name is: Jose Perez. Your new role: a job earning minimum wage at a store.

You live life as normally as possible. Friends, cousins, work, play. You send money home, as much as you can. Soon, you realize you need to make more money. You get a new name and part. You get a better job, one fixing cars. You love cars and have been fixing them since you were fourteen.

"The company hired me, once they saw me fix cars and all of my tools. Now I'm a doctor. A doctor of vehicles. I wear rubber gloves and the blood is dark brown. My uniform is grey with the name Richard on my shirt. And just like a doctor, I fix people's car by opening them up for $14 per hour."

Then, you meet a woman. You marry her and have a child, but she is kind of crazy. You end up in court—the real US Court—because your wife's brother was driving under the influence of heroin.

The judge asks you: "Sir, how did you get your residency?"

"Well ser, I went to la Pacific y la Eslauson, I saw the mica man. He asked me que necesitas, what do you need? And I told him, una licencia y seguro social. A driver's license and a social security number."

"What name did you take on?"

"You mean, what's my new acting name."

"Yes."

"Richard Sanchez."

"Do you have a steady job?"

"Yes, I work fifty plus hours per week and have people come to look for me. I also bring in my cousins and friends to fix their cars. Mexicans don't really trust mechanics."

You get deported to the Imperial Valley. Days later, you return, walking across at night just east of Calexico and go back to work as if you went on vacation.

You work day after day, fixing people's brakes, transmissions, *de todo*. You pay income taxes, state and federal, and sales tax, you pay rent, you buy a truck.

"I drive with insurance my cousin bought and drive safely. Cops shouldn't pull me over for no reason, I know my rights."

You hurt your back at work and settle out of court.

"I was retrained in computers and learned how to network. Even though my back hurts all the time, I still work on cars because I earn more money working on cars."

You pay child support now too. You pay, but she does not let you see your son. "I want to see my child."

The acting game continues, names change and vary for survival purposes. He—as do many others—hopes that one day, his real name is used. Until his existence is accepted on the big screen of America society, he will continue to change names for any big role in survival. For the time being, the current name works because somebody will always need his vehicle fixed.

Figure 19.1. "Pondering"

Chapter Nineteen

Tengo Coco

"Mira, tengo coco," my mother said as she pointed to her cerebro, to her hair, to her head, ultimately to her brain.

"Tengo coco." She repeated herself with a determination to prove that she and us Mexicans are not stupid people.

The conversation emerged from our discussion about my career and the lack of employment profession.

"Como te va el trabajo?"

"Igual, no avanso. Me considero exitoso si me dan clases ya ni trabajo fijo."

Looking for labor is worse than searching for that first fuck in one's life. La cojida seems hopeful, filling out these applications seems useless and repetitive. I often wonder if they really read the applications and letters of interest.

As I filled out yet another application, I scribbled in the information. Should my degrees not count for something other than how they look on a generic form that seemed no different than filing out a welfare form? At least, the welfare form actually resulted in something positive: money and food stamps. No matter how little the amount was, the end result was still positive. The county offices made sure no matter how humiliating their process was, people would receive a subsidy. Why not? Is America not about subsidizing their chosen ones?

This application for a full-time, permanent teaching job was a waste of time. There was no guarantee de nada. Why waste my valuable time? Toilet paper and baby wipes served more a purpose than an application for that country club job. My cynicism has proven true. For in my years of teaching as an adjunct professor, I have noticed that when people want to hire you, really hire you, you fill out the application after they have offered you the job.

On each of the applications, I filled out my frustration. In every cursive letter, I tell them fuck you, fuck you, fuck you with your pinche jale. A sort of subliminal graffiti, placazos, a fuck you vete a la chingada, hijos de tus chingada madre, vayan se a la verga, pinches putos. The tragedy of placazos is that we do it to our own neighborhoods instead of their villas.

As I have filled out endless applications at White community colleges such as Golden West, Long Beach City, El Camino, Mt. San Antonio and Fullerton in the greater Los Angeles and Orange County areas, I have realized I wrote my anger out and vented in every letter. They knew those letters were codices for fuck you, fuck you and fuck you, you White son of a bitches. And sure enough only one has had the courage of sending me a rejection. The others were so arrogant in their denial, they never sent any form of notification.

Community colleges are a great reason why all schools should be state wide districts just as the University of California or California State University system.

My mother could see that frustration in me. "Se los dan a gavachos y a otros grupos verdad?"

"They'll hire Whites first and other people from other groups."

"Si."

That was when she pointed to her head, and said, "Tengo coco."

No somos pendejos! We are not stupid, but the outside world believes we are.

The rest of California society, outsiders, American and immigrants believe they are smarter than us. All other Latinos want to correct our Spanish. They tell us that the way we Mexicans speak Spanish is incorrect, yet they lack the knowledge that we speak a Nahualt version of Spanish. And still, they feel they can correct us.

My ethnic teaching background makes me less than the traditional figure to teach history. But what qualifies them? After all, their approach is one sided; I at least have to merge both sides. Having a degree in history does not make a person a historian—working, living, reading, collecting data, recording oral histories, battling in society, those things make a person more knowledgeable and able to teach with some authority.

So, how do Mexicans overcome being considered stupid?

My mother has not been able to even though she knows southern California and Los Angeles history from having lived her 58 years of life here. She is still just a Mexican, and her minimum wage plus tips job of cutting hair and making up old ladies livable amounts to a wad of dollar bills, a wad which seems like it comes from dollar dance tips stuffed in between fake tits and bulging red lips blowing kisses.

Apart from tweaking her fingers, she is also known as a counselor. From the street, she is viewed as just another dumb Mexican, but among Mexicans, she is respected.

Pero pendeja mi mama no es? We just happen to live in a pendejo society.

My mother explained the racial caste structure for us Mexicans to me when I was younger, and I cannot say she encouraged me as our sighs coincided. We just comprehended that chingazos is all we know and chingazos we must give.

I sense that maybe in the after life I might find freedom to be the war-rior–both physically and intellectually that I am destined to be. Sometimes, when I sleep, I know I am dead as the aches of waking up hurt my head and force me to confront a society that believes I am dumb. Death is the great escape, especially as I wonder if I can handle thirty more years of pendijismo. I have no more goals, I am just on survival mode. I have no hope other than sleeping at night and coming into my life experiences.

I see my mother and await her passing, so I can move on too, for I do not want her to see me gone. She taught me to fight, but the energy of fighting is useless if they perceive me to be incompetent.

We Mexicans have two existences; thus, we live a double life in this society. Our White lives are about limitations, but in our world, we are valued. When we are free of American judgment, we are somebody.

Mi tio Pepe or Little Joe (as he was known) is a good example of a Mexican man who had two existences.

In my teenage years, I used to ride the brownish-orange limo called RTD. I would flip open my five dollar limo pass, and if I was fortunate, I rode home on a seat. On occasion as I would step up into the bus, I would see two feet hanging, almost dangling. I recognized those feet instantly. They were small, midget like. As I looked up, I greeted my great uncle (my mother's tio, first cousin of my grandfather Matias Segura Venegas and husband of my grandmother's sister). My tio little Joe was born in Kansas City, Missouri in 1918 and was named Jose Venegas.

During the era of Repatriation, the Americans expelled him and his family to the outskirts of Leon, Guanjuato. It was the 1930s, and he was a teenager who was fully bilingual. He was light years ahead of American educational standards. Here was a young man, born in the USA but sent away in one of history's massive panics of "Mexicans are taking our jobs away."

My tio Little Joe eventually returned north (a U.S. citizen who sneaked in before he could obtain a copy of his birth certificate) to California and resettled with other Venegas and Guerreros in Inglewood. Somewhere along his trajectory of life, he became a *sobador*, a healer, a Mexican style of chiropractor.

By the time, I was a teenager in the 1980s, I knew that if I had a sprained ankle or wrist o *la moyera caida, he was the sobador.* He was considered extraordinary, truly gifted. I knew he was unique and gifted because I saw many people go to him to be treated. He had people that sought him out in his small one bedroom duplex they rented.

In the old days before the city of Inglewood eminent-domained the last Mexican ranchos in the 1970s, they lived in more open space. It seemed that the more Inglewood became urban, the less space we Mexicans were permitted to occupy. This man of natural science barely had enough space to heal.

And still we went to him.

He would put a blue bandana around his head and always wore a Pendleton with his baggy pants. He would take a bottle of alcohol and pour some into them to wash his hands thoroughly. None of the rubbing alcohol was lost, he just seemed to cleanse his hands. After rubbing up and down, he would take your wrist or ankle and would put pressure and begin to sobar tightly creating heat.

Simultaneously, he mumbled something incomprehensible. He kept a serious look and seemed to be lost in a tiniebla, a gaze concentrated on his healing. I remember his hands became hot, but at the same time, a soothing sensation was felt by his hands. Once he finished, he quietly stated that the sobada should help. My tio Pepe would take his bandana off and would return to the conversation prior to the sobada. He seemed to have changed auras, from healing with a serious energy back to his Mexican American life of comadreo and smoking a cigarette. It was understood that that was a private ritual and private it remained.

When I would see him on the limo, with his gardening outfit and his bright orange "City of Lawndale" shirt where he was only a typical gardener and smelled like a football player, my tio Little Joe seemed like an average Mexican. A Mexican that cut somebody else's grass and who did not even earn enough pay to drive his own car as an older man. A sixty-plus year old gardener who rode the bus to and from work.

In the White world, he did what he was permitted to do. In the Mexican world, in the very space we all occupied, my tio Little Joe was a healer, un sobador who cured people.

Smart, I am, but what good is it to be clever if I am not valued on a societal level.

The minimal is all I will do.

We do have coco; however, this suicidal society fails to recognize that.

Chapter Twenty

Miami, Arizona

Mi tio, Amado, was one of those uncles who always seemed old and very quiet to me. Yet, there were times he would open up and laugh. His laugh was always a pleasure to hear because he chuckled with his whole chest and a cigarette in between his two fingers. What stood out the most was how white his teeth were and how dark his skin was. Mi tio had a beautiful dark chocolate hue with black, black hair, sideburns, a thick mustache, and a smile that went from one side of his face to the other.

Amado never seemed to age. He was a muscular man who had worked as a regador. A regador was a person who would wake up at 4 AM, put on sweaty, dirty pants that were only worn for field work and a long sleeve, cotton shirt and climb into black rubber rain boots that went up to his knees. He would pick up his shovel, his sombrero, and a gallon of water—off he was in his small pick up truck to water the agricultural fields south of Mexicali. He was the lifeline of these fields whether there was cotton, asparagus or even hay parcelas. He watered these fields by diverting canal ditches and then by opening those ditches. All by hand.

When I would shake my tio Amado's hand, I felt as though I was touching the worn out wooden handle from a shovel, his calluses were so hard. As I noticed the roughness of his hands that indicated he worked hard, I realized the softness of my hands also signified I did not work. If your hands are soft, you do not work. And I believe this to be true. I did not work, that was why I went to high school and college. I did not want to work.

Mi tio, Amado, was good to me. Maybe because when my father died, I would spend summers in Mexicali, he would talk to me calmly and in his own way reassure me. Mi tia Beva, (his wife) made me feel welcomed. My cousin, Toño, was my favorite of his children.

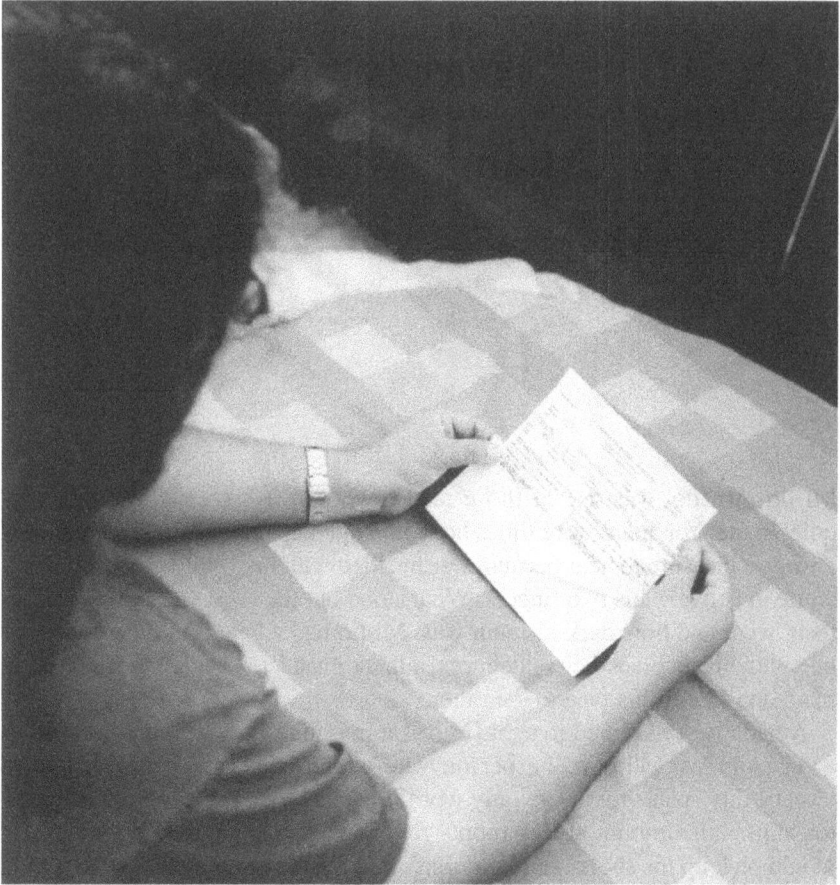

Figure 20.1.   "Looking at a Birth Certificate"

Mi tio Amado, was at times indifferent or only spoke when discipline had to be established; it was always Victor (his oldest son) who he was disciplining. My cousin, Toño, was the one who was always heckled by Victor. Yet, word has it through the others that Victor was a replica of Amado. My sister would tell me, Amado might be kind today, but there was a time when he would disappear on Beva and Victor (who was an infant); sometimes, he would be gone from three or six months. Amado would be brutal to my cousin Toño. But now that Toño has moved on to another world, Amado visits his son daily at the panteon, El Valle de los Recuerdos: The Valley of Memories Cemetery.

Mi tio, Amado, nonetheless is human, a human with a history himself. I remember him telling me about working in the agricultural fields of California in the 1960s, up and down the Sacramento and San Joaquin Valley picking grapes and other produce. He mentioned a couple of times being slave arrested by the migra, INS. I really did not pay much attention, maybe it was too much to handle or too overwhelming. Hearing talk about the fields for me was like being stabbed. I had seen this life from my paternal grandmother and hoped to stay away even from conversation. For me, there was nothing beautiful about the fields of California, just plain living racist hell and smelly bodies.

My mother was right, no Mexican or their offspring had a future if they continued to work in the fields. In the fields, you lost your body young and remained poor, plus you had to always worry about the migra. There was no dream in California, only a gavacho(gringo) crematory.

My tio told me that he would be gone for months, working up in northern California as an American slave. Getting deported and the suffocating Anglo culture was too much for Amado that by the late 1960s he stopped making tours. His three children were born in Mexicali, where they lived in an adobe home and where he felt the most comfortable and safe, out on the rancho.

That one summer of 1984 that I spent there at the Rancho Roa, I would accompany him to different places. One place was the local jail to visit a drunk who had accidentally burnt the junkyard he was taking care of. I could not believe that. A man was sent to jail for burning a junkyard. What was the big deal? The cars were junk anyway. Even if it was a yonkera, what did it matter, nobody was hurt. Nobody intentionally states, "I am going to burn a junkyard." It was an accident, even if he was drunk. I saw, off of the highway, the patch of land where the burning occurred, and I thought that it looked improved. Junkyards are eyesores, but according to the authorities, that was an open air auto parts store. And there was money to be made there. A junkyard is not just a junkyard in Baja California. So, the poor man remained in jail for four to five months for accidentally starting a fire probably from a campfire. We always had campfires in Mexicali, except camping was at home.

It turned out that the drunk that my tio, Amado, and I went to talk to was Echeverria, the husband of my father's older sister who roamed Mexicali as she was a mentally handicap woman. The coincidences of life. I had not met him until the year prior. He confessed to being the father of those cousins of mine from my tia Chepina.

Mi tio Amado gave Echeverria a couple of packs of Marlboro Red cigarettes through the metal fence separating us from the savagery of the jail. I felt fear as the door behind Echverria would open and close to let inmates see their visitors. It seemed that wickedness cried out as the doors opened and closed. As we left, mi tio Amado told him, "No se preocupe, nosotros nos preocuparemos por Chepina." Reassuring him about his mentally handicap wife, my tía.

As we walked out to the dusty road in central Mexicali and the gray of the night began to rise, I asked my tio about his background. I knew that he was born in Sinaloa, near Culiacan but had been in Mexicali most of his life. I knew Doña Chayo, his mother; in fact, I kind of considered her my abuela too. Yet I knew nothing of his father.

"Quien fue su papa?"

"Victor Moreno, el habia nacido en un pueblo llamado Miami, Arizona," my tio explained to me.

"Como?"

"Si, mi padre era nacido en Estados Unidos, el era cuidano Americano, y la familia de mi mama era de Santa Rosalia en Baja California."

I could not believe what I had heard. His father was an American citizen, born in Miami, Arizona. How was it then that he did not have his residency?

"Mi jefe se fue para Sinaloa y alla conocio a mi madre y yo naci, luego se separaron. Tuvo otra familia y despues nos contactamos otra ves. Pero de distancia. Supe que el ahora estaba invalido en un hospital aqui en el valle, en El Centro (across the line on the USA side)," he continued.

I then got to thinking: why was he undocumented? He entered quietly to not be detected, but by his father's birth, he should have been a USA citizen born abroad. He should not have been rounded up like a wild Mexican by the INS. Plus, he could have provided US residency to his sons and daughter. He remained quiet about his father as we drove home. All I thought about were his days in central California being treated as a "Mexican"—fearful of captivity and his inability to get his rightful American citizenship.

Mi tio, Amado, never acquired his citizenship, nor does he have a social security number from his ten years of seasonal work in the fields. More importantly, his son, Victor Moreno, has never been able to obtain his residency owed to him by birth. In the late 1980s, Victor Moreno, son of Amado and grandson of an American citizen, entered the USA on a work permit and renewed it annually. For six or seven years, he worked in roofing in Los Angeles, in Minnesota, in upstate New York, and in the Imperial Valley. Then, one day when he applied for his renewal, an INS agent refused, his work permit was stolen by an INS agent in Calexico. The agent escorted him out of the building—as if never needed again. Since then, he has been desperately trying to come over but is afraid to do so as an undocumented.

He was not needed anymore and expelled even though his grandfather was an American citizen born in Miami, Arizona, born as his father built the railroad, the same railroad used today in commerce, so vital to our economy.

The last time I saw my tio, Amado, was at my abuela's funeral. He asked me, "Do you think you could inquire about getting my father's social security number? I was told by an attorney that if I can get his social security, I can at least get my American citizenship and go work a few years al otro lado. The attorney told me there are too many Victor Morenos to try to match."

I tried to no avail.

No Mexican—even if born in the United States—is guaranteed of his rights and due process under the law.

Not even a citizen of the US by birth. Not even a citizen.

Figure 21.1. "Boys Playing Cars"

Chapter Twenty-one

Brandon y Bebo

In the Jardines del Desierto, Mexicali, in April of 2004, JoséAlfredo Jimenez was blasting out of my black 1999 Ford Expedition. The words "La vida no vale nada, la vida no vale nada" kept echoing even though that song, "Caminos de Guanajuato" had ended seven songs back.

The white casket remained open, glass cover under the yucateco tree. The afternoon sun warmed the flat Mexicali cemetery. My grandfather's tomb had been opened to make room for his wife. I never recall my grandparents sleeping in the same bed during my 34-year life span, but now they were going to spend an eternity on top of each other in an eight by four foot hole. The casket remained open for one last time. Not so much for my grandmother, for she was resting eternally, rather for us.

This family of little wealth, few educational, or political accomplishments, would continue to live only to quarrel and be divided by personalities and suffer la chingada vida. Even in this death, our animosity towards one another did not allow us to grief collectively. One tia stayed away from another, my mother from her brother and sister-in-law, one primo from another. At times, I felt my mother kept away from me, but she was keeping her distance from my paternal grandmother. If my brother was there, he and my brother-in-law would have been ignoring each other, all the while straining my sister's energy.

I too joined the circus; I avoided my tio and his imposing wife, smiling and grinding my teeth. I kept my distance from my drinking cousins beyond *Epas'* with their heads tilting back as a greeting. Also on my list were some second cousins who I do not care for. I too hold a grudge eternally for being mistreated as a teenager. Self-imposed distance is my remedy even in times of mourning.

Nobody ever plans funerals; they just happen even in the midst of a wedding. My brother was getting married exactly at the same time my grandmother's body was deposited in the earth, never knowing she had died.

Maybe mi'ama was happy to go. Who can handle so many personalities? She had created directly or indirectly more than thirty people, and yet at times I know she wish she had not. Peacefully, she was gone, even if to flee this chaos. If these people, her offspring fought with no inheritance involved, imagine the horrible ordeals if inheritance was an issue. Maybe it was best for her to leave. There would never be peace. There was neither tranquility or a sense of decency on account of sibling rivalry and even adult grandchildren who imposed their wants at the expense of others.

Who knows, maybe this was nature? Nature in and of itself is diverse. There are many land forms, many different types of flowers and plants, many unique types of animals with their own distinctive sub type. Why are two legged animals unique?

Personality differences were so extreme in my family that during a word session at mi'ama's funeral, my tia Lupe stated, "Ya no nos vamos a ver juntos," with teary eyes for her mother. Perhaps, she vented her fear that there would never be a reunion again. Our linkage was gone, there she lay in a white box with a glass cover over her, adorned with coronas and other flower stands as if a veil.

The time neared, miama Alberta to be interned. Her favorite singer, José Alfredo, sounded intrusive, so I went to turn it off. As I walked around the mounted soil that would claim her to the earth and the other tumbas, I walked toward the front of the vehicle for the back was opened to the crowd. Twenty feet away, distanced from open unused future cemetery soil, I paused for a moment; next to a 1970 Chevrolet Truck under a mesquite tree, two boys played oblivious to their great-grandmother's internment.

They played on their knees like mammals with their trucks in their hands, making swirls of dust. There, they played in a place of grievance under the guise of Don José, my brother-in-law's father, who supervised and perhaps pondered when he was next. We all die sooner or later.

In the midst of all this commotion, these two boys played, Bebo and Brandon, the sons of my cousins Sofia from Mexicali and Sandra from Wilmington. My eyes stared in amazement, in comfort, in hope of life. I couldn't help but stare: Brandon would yell, *Bebo*, in his American accent. Brandon did not speak Spanish. Americanization had rooted out Mexico from Brandon, yet if not for his English, most would assume that Brandon was from Mexicali, but maybe not, Mexicans in Mexico do not use the name Brandon.

Brandon kept playing in the dirt talking to his Mexican cousin who did not speak English. Bebo would ask, "Brandon? Spsspspspspspsspp, el que habla asi." And there, these cousins who did not speak the same language but shared the same great-grandmother played. Somehow, they managed to communicate joyfully while others were soon to never see each other again.

The internment neared, but I kept watching Brandon and Bebo laughing and driving their small metal cars in a circle on the dirt.

A vendor passed by and I stated: "Mira esos, sin preocupacion de la vida."

The vendedor who made a living by selling raspados to the mourners understood my concern, and said: "Son el futuro, son el futuro."

Finally, I turned away from them and returned to the funeral in progress under the yucateco tree. Slowly, mi'ama was lowered into her womb with her husband forever.

Those boys are the future, they are the future. With those words of wisdom, I felt a sense of compassion, a sense of wisdom that their future, the future has hope. An optimism in two children playing as one, not understanding each other's language yet nonetheless content about playing with one another. Even as our family died, we hadn't. Our children give us hope. Our lives will remain eternal as if always playing in the swirls of dust.

We must live in two worlds, we must fight this suicidal society. We must force our truth to be told. We must have hope in the future, hope that what we say and do matters.

www.ingramcontent.com/pod-product-compliance
Lightning Source LLC
Chambersburg PA
CBHW050526280326
41932CB00014B/2473